ABOUT THE BOOK

In *Solving the American Healthcare Crisis: (Improving Value via Higher Quality and Lower Costs by Aligning Stakeholders)*, Dr. Robert J. Cerfolio, MD, MBA, asserts that the mutual distrust between Democrats and Republicans has hit new levels and has paralyzed us—preventing us from solving the crisis of the United States' healthcare system. The focus of conversation has become juvenile political insults as opposed to the language of leaders who seek mature, innovative solutions. Meanwhile, in the greatest and most caring country in the world, many innocent Americans fail to receive the treatment they need and deserve. Still, we have the highest quality healthcare system in the world—it may not provide the best value, but it does provide the best quality.

In *Solving the American Healthcare Crisis*, Dr. Cerfolio discusses innovative and practical solutions to such problems as providing high-quality health care and motivating physicians, patients, and insurance companies alike to invest in preventive care. Improving our healthcare system is not about supporting any political party, but rather about understanding the strengths and weaknesses in what each party proposes. He suggests that the best solution lies somewhere in the middle—and in the spirit of innovation, choice, and free-market competition.

Bigger government is not the answer, and neither is a single private payer—but denying American citizens health care is wrong and immoral.

First, we must agree upon whether health care is a right or a privilege. Dr. Cerfolio asserts that it is a right of every legal American citizen. Regardless of race, creed, religion, beliefs, or sexual orientation, every single American—upon birth or citizenship—deserves and must receive high-quality health care.

These are the values that represent my values and those of a caring society. Indeed, it is what the United States of America represents to the entire world—even today, despite our current political strife. Nearly every physician, and most insurance companies and hospitals, agree to take care of the indigent. Few Americans are aware of these facts. Few know that the emergency room staff and doctors and nurses have already been providing care for these patients for years.

Quality over volume is the new buzz word and culture for medical providers. In the past we as physicians and providers have been paid for volume of care as opposed to quality of care. However, there remains confusion and great controversy as to what is value and who is best to judge it: the patient, the payer, the provider or another stakeholder such as medical or surgical societies. Moreover, how is it best quantified and risk-stratified? Cerfolio will show that value and quality are objective terms that are determined by the formula:

$$Value = Quality\ /\ cost$$

He has studied and extensively lectured and written about how to improve value by decreasing cost. This part of the equation is not a major focus of this book since physicians and administrator have thousands of finished and other ongoing projects that are continually reducing the cost of healthcare via the process of Lean and other novels strategies. However, value and quality must share the same unit as cost – ie dollars – thus quality has to be objectified and monetized accurately. We and others have already shown ways to put a price tag on readmissions, returns to the operating room to treat a complication and most importantly not practicing effective preventive care.

There are many obstacles to the ultimate goal of high-quality health care for all US citizens at a low cost; the largest is the lack of alignment among the current stakeholders in our healthcare system. Patients are not aligned in their own health. They pay about the same whether they are in great shape or not, and physicians, hospitals, and insurance companies make more money when patients are sick instead of healthy. We are de-incentivized for Americans to be healthy. High-functioning, complex teams succeed only when all of the teammates and stakeholders are aligned and share similar metrics. This is a cornerstone of our solution.

Recently, there has been much controversy over the coverage of pre-existing conditions. The entire debate is mal-aligned and mis-defined. Many of these conditions are not "preexisting conditions," but rather are conditions that would be better labelled as "consequential conditions," secondary to poor choices. Liver failure from alcohol abuse, advanced emphysema from smoking, and diabetes and joint pain from obesity are just a few examples. Americans have to own these choices, since most are made freely. Thus, Americans should pay more for them, just as we do in every other facet of our lives. Children who are born and raised in social circumstances that almost force poor choices upon them are different. A caring and loving society—which is what we the USA—should take care of all of our children, regardless of their pathology or "consequential conditions," since many were placed in situations over which they had no free choice or control. However, at some point, children become adults and are then responsible for their choices, despite a challenging upbringing. Everyone knows that smoking is not good, but we need to provide addiction clinics to help those who want to stop smoking.

Dr. Cerfolio describes how we are closer to solutions than many think, because we have engaged in some of the required productive dialogue about the challenges and solutions to health care. In *Solving the American Healthcare Crisis*, Dr. Cerfolio advances this conversation, bringing us closer to the future of health and wellness in the United States by aligning all the stakeholders from both ends of the healthcare payment teeter-totter.

ABOUT THE AUTHOR

Robert J. Cerfolio, MD, MBA, is an academic thoracic surgeon and an international thought-leader in innovative care to lower the cost and improve the quality of surgery and health care. He has performed more than 17,700 operations at the University of Alabama, Birmingham, as the James H. Estes Family Lung Cancer Research Endowed Chair and Chief of Thoracic Surgery and Chair of the Business Intelligence Team. He has recently accepted the role of Professor at the New York University Langone Medical Center, now relabeled New York Langone Health. Dr. Cerfolio is now the Professor of Cardio-Thoracic Surgery and Chief of the Clinical Division of Thoracic Surgery at New York University Langone Medical Center. He is also the Inaugural Director of the Lung Cancer Service Line for the Perlmutter Cancer Center at NYU and the Senior Director and Advisor of the Robotics Program. Additionally, he serves many national and international roles, including the Director of the American Association of Thoracic Surgery's Robotic Graham Fellowship and Training Program.

Dr. Cerfolio's innovative robotic and other surgical techniques have reduced complications, increased survival rates, and shortened hospital stays. He has taught his techniques to more than 1,200 national and international surgeons, anes-thesiologists, and their teams and has operated as a visiting professor in many countries. He also has published more than 170 original, peer-reviewed articles and fifty book chapters, and has delivered more than 430 lectures and presentations at major national and international scientific meetings.

Dr. Cerfolio has published articles on the process of lean—which is the reduction of wasteful, non-valued steps to a process as well as value stream mapping and root cause analysis. He has brought many business models and concepts to the patient's bedside and not only dramatically improved the care of patients, reduced pain and recovery time, but also improved customer service, reduced waiting time via telemedicine, and reduced the cost of delivering higher quality care.

Solving the American Healthcare Crisis: (Improving Value via Higher Quality and Lower Costs by Aligning Stakeholders) is Dr. Cerfolio's third book. The first, *Super Performing at Work and Home – The Athleticism of Surgery*, delivers the message of work-life balance. It relates stories of lessons learned from Dr. Cerfolio's collegiate athletic career as a First Team Academic All-American Baseball player and the humility and helpless-ness of watching his wife of twenty-one years lose her battle to leukemia caused by chemotherapy she had received three years earlier for Stage II breast cancer.

Dr. Cerfolio's second book, entitled *Inspire*, relates leadership lessons. Dr. Cerfolio has written these books while maintaining a busy surgical schedule and national and international travel lecture schedule. He believes in the collective leadership ability of US citizens and our culture and process. He believes that together—united as one and not divided by the archaic mindset of the second millennium that divide us by race, religion, sexual orientation, or bigotry—we can further improve our healthcare system from what already is one of the best in the world, to the best.

SOLVING THE AMERICAN
HEALTHCARE
CRISIS

SOLVING THE AMERICAN HEALTHCARE CRISIS

IMPROVING VALUE VIA HIGHER QUALITY AND LOWER COSTS BY ALIGNING ALL STAKEHOLDERS

Robert J. Cerfolio, MD, MBA

Printed in the United States of America

Library of Congress Control Number: 2017959773

ISBN Paperback: 978-1-947368-38-5
ISBN eBook: 978-1-947368-39-2

Interior Design: Ghislain Viau

CONTENTS

INTRODUCTION

Every aspect of the highly politicized conversation about our healthcare system seems to emphasize the mutual distrust between Democrats and Republicans, instead of being about ways to provide the most efficient care at the lowest cost. This contentious atmosphere prevents us from overcoming our current challenges with a solutions-oriented approach. The national split has grown wider, and with the widening of that divide, the solution to health care is further away.

Why I Have Written this Book

As a viewer from afar, I have grown more than tired of the political discourse, the immature tat for tat, the personal attacks, the juvenile tweets, and the second-grade-level leadership of our broken political system. As I tell my three boys every day: Don't complain about things. Be the person who provides solutions. Be a true leader and fix the problems. My sons, in return, have challenged me with, "Dad, fix the national healthcare crisis! Stop complaining about it." Thus, I have written this book to discuss practical solutions to such problems as providing universal access to health care and motivating physicians, patients, and insurance companies alike to invest in preventive care.

I am an academic thoracic (chest) surgeon, so you may be wondering why I'm writing about preventive health and population health care. After all, my typical patient is not an uninsured person who suffers from chronic disease. My typical patient is a wealthy, highly educated individual who has searched for the best care. Some have traveled from other countries to get the highest quality lung or esophageal cancer surgery and oncologic care in the world. These are not the patients who need better care in the USA.

My education—including my MBA from the University of Tennessee, which specializes in MBAs for MDs—and my medical experience might provide a unique insight into our current situation, which allows for ideas on possible solutions.

I am a surgical specialist who further sub-specializes in lung and esophageal cancer surgery. I have performed more than 17,700 operations in the US during my time at the University of Alabama at Birmingham, and now more recently at New York University. I have been a visiting professor at many other famous hospitals all over the world. Although I am in academic medicine, many jokingly say that I run one of the world's largest private practices. I currently serve as a Professor of Cardio-Thoracic Surgery and Chief of the Clinical Division of Thoracic Surgery at New York University Langone Medical Center.

I am also the Inaugural Director of the Lung Cancer Service Line for the Perlmutter Cancer Center at NYU. This latter title is significant because *service lines* are the future of patient care. Service lines break down the silos of divisional finances and align hospital and physician finances with patient concerns—getting the best care at the lowest cost that is most convenient for the patient, from whatever specialist and tests best serve the patient's specific needs.

Let me explain what this means to patients. Right now, a surgeon only gets paid if he or she operates on you. I truly believe that 99 percent of us only operate when the patient needs surgery—but at the end of the day, we are incentivized to operate. If there is a better way to care for you that does *not* entail surgery, then we do not make any money.

The goal of a service line is to change that dynamic. The service line is a group of physicians who are surgeons, medical oncologists (doctors who give chemotherapy), radiation oncologists, and pulmonologists (lung specialists). If we share finances, then we have an incentive to provide you with the best care at the lowest cost. In theory, we share the profits. However, few service lines in the United States in the arena of cancer truly profit-share.

My academic credentials—more than two hundred peer-reviewed articles published, more than sixty book chapters, and more than four hundred and fifty lectures as a visiting professor or invited speaker in at least twenty countries—have provided me with insight and perhaps given me a platform. My wide-ranging professional travel has exposed me to many different political and social approaches to health care.

I know we can modify our healthcare system to increase efficiency and effectiveness and to become more patient-focused. But first, it is important to recognize that politicizing health care hinders its progress, because it shifts the focus *away from* providing the best care at the lowest cost. Improving our healthcare system is not about supporting the political party we associate with; it's about understanding that strengths and weaknesses are inherent in each party's proposals. The best solution will lie somewhere in the middle.

Many conversations today are about employing the healthcare models of other countries, like Canada or various European nations. People are under the impression that health care in these countries is cheaper and more efficient. Having operated and lectured in many countries in the last several years, I've had firsthand experience with these healthcare models.

The reality is that the majority of people I encounter abroad admire the US healthcare system, especially our quality. And many of those countries are moving toward our system as we, ironically, are moving more toward a more socialistic system. While we have higher premiums and greater administrative costs, we generally also see better results in the form of improved quality of life and lives saved. In fact, an American Cancer Society report states that the cancer death rate in the US has steadily declined in the last twenty years and is now 25 percent lower than it was in 1991.[1]

Don't be fooled by the many one-line graphs and charts that show lower cancer survival rates in the US compared to other countries. Each set of data is collected and defined differently, and some are just not accurate because they compare apples to oranges. The image below, used by Cancer Research UK, shows that the United States, among other countries, has higher-than-average incidence of cancer.[2] Is this really true?

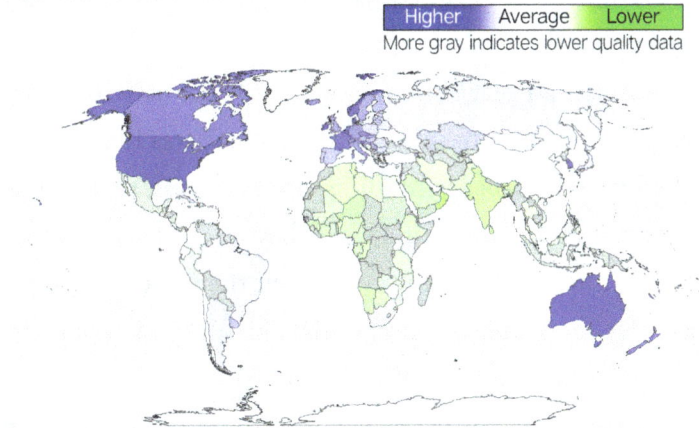

Cancer Incidence Worldwide

Higher Average Lower
More gray indicates lower quality data

---

1 https://www.cancer.org/latest-news/cancer-facts-and-figures-death-rate-down-25-since-1991.html

2 http://www.cancerresearchuk.org/health-professional/cancer-statistics/worldwide-cancer/mortality#collapseZero

Could it be that we have more people going through screening programs for prostate, colon, breast, and lung cancers? Is the data really accurate and comparing similar groups?

The international Communist and socialist healthcare systems that I have experienced are shifting to a more capitalistic healthcare model, similar to ours. When health care is given freely, it tends to be less effective because everyone involved is not incentivized to provide and expect high quality. I have not meet a single doctor who works in our VA systems who, when answering candidly, does not admit this fact. For example, physicians who are not paid per procedure will perform two surgeries a day instead of five, so patients wait longer. Further, some of their patients will not fully appreciate the level of care they are receiving, because they are not invested in it to a degree that establishes expectation.

I noticed a great example of this principle when I was leaving my hotel room this morning: There was free coffee in the lobby, and people were filling up their cups, taking a few sips, and then throwing it away. They didn't have anything invested in the coffee. However, when the same person goes to a coffee shop and pays four dollars for a cup of coffee, they don't spill a drop. They will drink it all down.

The principles of investment and incentive are the same within the healthcare industry. Healthcare reform thought leaders often say we need to be more like Canada, or that healthcare reform will mean less access to health care for more people. These statements are not true. In fact, I hesitate even to refer to these speakers as "experts" because they are not working on the front line; they have never seen or cared for patients. They have never operated for hours and been up all night in an ICU caring for and praying for patients. In addition, they don't have the data on the true economic impact of the plans they propose. Health care is a complex problem.

I recently operated on a man who had paid out-of-pocket to fly to the US from Canada to have me remove his lung cancer. He told me that, in Canada, he would have had to wait for months for that surgery. While many people cannot afford to come here for the services they need, many services cannot wait that length of time, either. Canada's healthcare system is good—actually *very* good—and it is getting better. I'm sure some Canadian physicians reading this don't believe the patient was right about the wait he expected to have—but this was his truth and his statement to us.

Though our healthcare system needs improvement, it's not the worst in the developed world, and we don't need to completely change our system to mimic those of other countries. In fact, we can't do that, because cultural differences lead to different values and goals in the US, and our politics lead to different processes. Still, the goal is universal: the highest quality care for all patients at the lowest cost.

If we can fly to the moon and Mars, we can figure out health care. In fact, we're closer to solutions than many think, because we are beginning to engage in more productive dialogue about the challenges and possibilities of health care.

I am writing this book because I believe in the incredible talents, creativity, and intelligence of US citizens and leaders. I believe in our collective ability to create a truly progressive healthcare system—once we put politics aside. But first, we have to stop the silly political party dialogue and act like elected politicians.

We can solve our healthcare problem together as a team—the *US* team—only if we are not the red or blue states, but the United States.

Chapter 1

HOW'D WE GET INTO THIS MESS?

THE FIRST STEP TOWARD A SOLUTION TO THE problems in our healthcare system is to understand our current situation. The politicization of our healthcare system began more than a century ago, and it continues to impede progress toward national access to high-quality, low-cost health care.

It is often helpful to know the history of a culture prior to trying to change a culture. Currently, our leaders seem to care about claiming which side solved a problem or fixed a problem or caused a problem—but not about actually providing solutions to the problem.

A Brief History of Health Care in the US

- In the early 1900s, families took care of their sick and paid the town doctor out of their own pockets. Hospitals, as we know them today, did not exist. But people could not always afford the expense of health care.

- In 1905, the American Association for Labor Legislation (AALL) was founded as an advocacy group for national health insurance in the United States.[1] They were a group of progressive activists who sought to reform health care while preserving its capitalist model.[2]

- From 1912–1915, the AALL unsuccessfully introduced healthcare initiatives, which gave rise to controversy about national insurance. By 1914, the American Medical Association (AMA) supported the AALL, while the American Federation of Labor (AFL) opposed it.[3]

- In 1917, the US entered WWI, and our involvement in this conflict gave rise to anti-socialist and anti-Communist sentiments. The AMA adamantly pushed against national health insurance, stating publically that it was too similar to Communism. However, perhaps the real reason the AMA opposed national health insurance was that physicians were afraid the government was going to restrict their fees, causing them to lose money.

---

1 https://en.wikipedia.org/wiki/American_Association_for_Labor_Legislation
2 http://www.pnhp.org/facts/a-brief-history-universal-health-care-efforts-in-the-us
3 http://www.pnhp.org/facts/a-brief-history-universal-health-care-efforts-in-the-us

- By the mid-1920s, people had begun using hospitals for x-rays, lab work, and other emerging medical procedures.

- In 1929, Blue Cross was established, with a business model based on a prototype plan developed by Justin Ford Kimball at Baylor University in Dallas, Texas.[4]

- In 1939, The American Hospital Association (AHA) wanted to increase the prevalence of prepaid health plans. They adopted the Blue Cross logo to designate plans that met their standards.

- During WWII, the government tried to ward off a post-war recession by providing tax incentives. In 1943, the IRS decided to offer employers tax deductions if they provided health care to their employees.[5] This was a critical moment in time and perhaps the single most important law in the history of American health care. This tax deduction characterizes our current culture and is part of what differentiates US health care from systems in most other countries. Employers responded by creating and operating their own, in-house insurance plans. They took healthcare premiums directly from employee paychecks (ensuring 100 percent payment), rather than contracting with insurance companies as

---

4 Blue Cross website: https://www.bcbs.com/learn/bcbs-blog/health-insurance-invention-innovation-history-blue-cross-and-blue-shield-companies#.U3-J2vldU7U

5 http://www.npr.org/templates/story/story.php?storyId=114045132

they do today. Thus, prepaid health insurance plans became more common.

- In 1945, President Harry Truman advocated for national health insurance, but the AMA again opposed it.

- In 1954, a law was passed that made the employer health-care tax advantages even more attractive. The government began to allow Blue Cross to operate as a tax-exempt, non-profit organization. When doctors realized the monetary benefits Blue Cross was reaping, they created their own prepaid health insurance plans and formed Blue Shield.

- By 1955, insurance coverage had spread to nearly 70 percent of the population—up from only 10 percent in 1940, a dramatic increase in just fifteen years. From the 1940s to the 1950s, the number of Americans who had private health insurance went from 20 million to 143 million. Blue Cross and Blue Shield were now paying hospitals and doctors directly, and all these stakeholders began to earn more money as they expanded their services. Ultimately, these prepaid insurance plans evolved into a fee-for-service model. Physicians were now paid to do *more*, rather than to deliver higher quality care. The fee-for-service model was lucrative for insurance companies and doctors. Private companies, hospitals, doctors, and patients all thrived in this environment.

- By 1965, the government wanted to ensure at least a minimal level of health care for all citizens. Medicaid was created for people with limited resources, and Medicare was created for people over the age of sixty-five. This was the beginning of the two-tiered system we have today—private *and* government-funded insurance. The government selected Blue Cross and Blue Shield to help them administer these programs.

- From 1965 to 1975, the share of health care paid by third parties went from 45 percent to 67 percent. Medicaid and Medicare were now reimbursing providers on a fee-for-service basis. Now there was *no* incentive to keep people healthy or to keep people out of the hospital—because the more patients they admitted, the more money hospitals and physicians made. This is the opposite of what this book will suggest as the solution for health care. My suggestion will involve more money for doctors and insurance companies when they have fewer sick people. I believe we must align the interests of healthcare providers so that they make more money when patients require fewer interventions.

- When President Carter took office in 1977, he tried to introduce a national health insurance program, but his idea was rejected by Congress. At that point, taxes were going up, and unemployment and inflation were on the rise. These circumstances led to Carter's 1980 presidential defeat at the hands of Ronald Reagan, who believed that the key to reducing healthcare costs was less government interference in the free market. The VA system was an archetypical example of a government-run health system—poor quality, long waits, unhappy patients, and unengaged staff members who worked shift hours and had more benefits than other employees—including early retirement perks. The deregulation of health care during the Reagan administration was successful for a time.

• From 1980 to 1986, for-profit, managed-care plans successfully decreased the cost of medical care. But by 1990, healthcare costs were on the rise again.

In the past, employers got a tax break for supplying health care to employees, and they could afford to do it—but that's no longer true. We're in our current situation because employers can't afford to keep paying for our health care, and hospital systems and physicians have no stake in controlling the cost of care. Excessive waste in health care has been tolerated because profit margins were so high that there was little need to bring costs down by eliminating inefficiency. Employers have taken all the advantages they can from providing health care, and companies are now attempting to implement a variety of strategies to work around rising costs.

One employer strategy for combating a poor economy would be to shift the costs of health care to employees. As costs continue to increase, employers will keep pushing for employees to pay a higher portion of their premiums. We have seen a skyrocketing in high-deductible packages over the past few years because of this phenomenon. As a result, employees pay higher premiums as well as larger deductibles and copays.

The other strategy is for employers to cut wages so they can afford to offer healthcare benefits. This option is frequently suggested, but it's never well received by the public. Some employers simply decide to get out of the healthcare business; they stop offering healthcare benefits to their employees.

With fewer employers offering health care, the Obama administration implemented the Patient Protection and Affordable Care Act (also known as Obama Care) in 2010, so that everyone would have access to health care. The goal is laudable and should be the goal of any proposed solution. Although the concept was a good one, many states have found the ACA to be unsustainable in its current form. The reality is that, to care for all of our citizens, another solution is sorely needed.

In Conclusion

How did we get into this mess? The problem is that, any time you have a third-party payer like an insurance company, administrative costs go up. If I cut your lawn, I would charge you directly—but if I perform an operation in a hospital, I have to go to Aetna to get the money. Why can't I just charge the patient directly? The answer is, it's too expensive (even though the surgeon's fee is only about 5 percent of the total surgery bill). Patients need insurance because they can't afford health care without it—but it would cost *less* if we didn't have the third party involved.

Large health insurance companies are extremely profitable and employ millions of Americans. Though it is likely that the type of third-party payers we have today will consolidate and then slowly be phased out and/or evolve, it is important to recognize that this won't be an immediate process and it won't provide an immediate solution, because of the large number of people and the large amount money involved in this side of the healthcare business.

Physicians are wrong when they blame third-party payers and insurance companies. Third-party payers provide great value: they help down some of the physicians' costs, such as the tests they order and the bills they submit. Additionally, they will eventually consolidate care to "centers of excellence," which will force lower-quality hospitals to go belly-up (something that is happening every day in the US).

The greatest strength of the Obama Care initiative was its ultimate goal: to ensure that everyone had access to health care. The problem is that the Obama administration put too much emphasis on the role of the federal government, rather than allowing the individual states to find novel ways to provide health care themselves.

The high level of government involvement not only increased taxes, but it pushed physicians, nurses, administrators, and hospital staff into a situation in which they were there to punch a clock and go home. Although it may not be politically correct to suggest that government involvement in an industry leads to high cost and poor quality, most physicians who have worked in the VA system know this is true. Is the post office—another government-run entity—any different?

With an employee mentality, no one is interested in taking on extra cases or going above and beyond in the level of care they provide. There's no incentive because they aren't invested in it. While you can't really punish people for not being good, you *can* provide bonuses so that people have an incentive to excel.

The Trump administration is correct in saying that aspects of our current system need revamping. If we don't fix Obama Care now, our healthcare system will become bankrupt. The reality is that Obama Care is already gone.

But the Trump administration has yet to propose the specific changes that would actually provide national access to high-quality, cost-effective health care. The topic has become so political—Republican versus Democrat—that the Trump plan does not stand a chance, regardless of its contents.

Democrats are going to say that Republicans are protecting high-profits for big business. They'll claim the Republican bill fails to provide healthcare access to everyone and does not require insurers to accept patients with pre-existing conditions.

The Republicans are going to say that the Democrats are too liberal and will run up exorbitant bills. They'll claim the Democrats are giving away free health care to people who don't pay taxes, and so on. Neither party will address the number of people—many of whom I have taken care of and operated on—who are on Medicaid even though they do not have a limiting physical disability.

Obviously, the answer is somewhere in the middle. What we need is a bipartisan bill and a wholesale cultural change in the process of arriving at solutions. It is doubtful that, in the current political milieu, we will be capable of coming to a sensible agreement. Perhaps the most frustrating part, for physicians and everyone else, is watching grown men and women act like children while real patients suffer every day.

It is certain that things are going to change, because our current situation is not sustainable. Part of the solution would be to have a system with more options—giving people the choice to opt out of Medicare, for example. Why should the government take money out of our paychecks and then decide what we spend on health care later in life? What if we were able to opt out of Medicare and choose to pay for health care on our own, through private insurance? Could we even be refunded the money the government has taken out of our paychecks in the past? Those who did not want to purchase their own insurance could continue to use government-funded health care.

The key is to provide more options. The key is choice. Flexibility allows the best to rise to the top. If Medicare is so good, why is it mandated? The same can be said of Obama Care. The goal of any option is to make it so good that people are *willing* to choose it.

Chapter 2

FOLLOW THE MONEY

To HAVE A PRODUCTIVE CONVERSATION ABOUT our current healthcare problems, we must first decide whether health care is a right or a privilege. We need to develop a shared vision of health care before we can create a system that meets the goal of providing cost-effective, high-quality care.

We must ask: Is health care a business? Is health care something that everyone should have? Should we make money from health care?

My opinion is that health care is a right that every American should have—*everyone*—but healthcare providers should be able to make money via the free market, thus forcing them to provide it better than their competition, with higher quality at a lower cost. Finally, people who make poor choices must pay more for health care.

The reality is that health care *is* a business. The problem is that all of the stakeholders—physicians, insurance companies, hospitals, and patients—are not aligned on what this means and how best to implement it.

For example, physicians often complain about insurance companies, yet insurance companies have real value in our current healthcare system. Insurance keeps costs down by making sure that doctors don't overcharge or, as described previously, by forcing physicians to follows pathways to reduce costs.

Physicians complain about insurance companies because of the inordinate amount of documentation and paperwork they require, the administrative costs, and so on. And it is true, this has gone too far. Many physicians are fed up with their practice because of these burdens.

But we physicians (some of us, anyway) got ourselves into this situation by ordering unnecessary tests that patients did not need, in medical centers in which we had shared ownership—in order to increase our own incomes.

Hospitals both benefit from and struggle with insurance companies. Currently, there is friction among all stakeholders. When teammates do not share the same values—when we are not aligned financially and/or emotionally—the outcomes of any team are less favorable.

The Business of Health Care

The insurance companies are in business to make a profit. And the truth is, physicians and hospitals are *also* in business to make a profit; this just isn't generally said, because of the common notion that one cannot serve the patient *and* be in favor of making a profit. But the two are not mutually exclusive.

As a physician, I am biased, because I know that the vast majority of doctors really do what is in the patient's best interest. The Hippocratic Oath that we stand and recite means so much to us, the responsibility we feel while taking it and practicing it every day is difficult to describe. However, we also want to get paid as much as possible, just like anybody else.

While health care is a business, the vast majority of the stakeholders—including insurance companies and industry— put the customer ahead of their profit margin. This is because our customers are sick and vulnerable. Hospitals, for example, do this every day: five to ten percent of my patients don't have insurance, but the hospital doesn't tell me that I can't operate on them or care for them. Insurance companies do the same.

Generally, stakeholders in the healthcare industry help patients even when those stakeholders are not turning a profit. In that sense, health care is not run like most businesses. When was the last time someone let you walk out of a store with a television that you could not afford?

Yet the healthcare industry is continually criticized for finding ways to sustain itself. Hospitals lose money by treating Medicaid patients, which is not a sustainable situation. In fact, hospitals are constantly closing down; it is estimated that one-third of the hospitals in the US will have closed by

2020.[1] Medical centers need more privately insured patients to make up for the financial loss incurred from treating Medicaid patients. Privately insured patients are necessary for hospitals to stay in business.

John Noseworthy, the CEO of the Mayo Clinic, recently said his clinic should prioritize privately insured patients over Medicaid or Medicare patients. He did not say the Mayo Clinic was going to *deny* care to Medicaid patients. He did not say they would not provide the same excellent care for all of their patients. He just stated that, if two patients call at the same time, the one with private insurance should get preference.

Noseworthy's statement has since been blown out of proportion, and he has experienced major backlash.[2] The Mayo Clinic has more than 35,000 employees to pay—which they can't do if they're losing money. Without income, they can't take care of any patients, either. As I always say, "No money, no mission."

To resolve such issues, many are now suggesting that government-funded healthcare programs should replace private insurers. It has been argued that private insurance companies are more expensive than Medicare. This is an argument for switching to a single federal payer—the "single payer" argument. However, the image below[3] demonstrates that

1 http://www.kevinmd.com/blog/2012/03/onethird-hospitals-close-2020.html
2 The *Washington Times*, Friday, March 17, 2017: http://www.washingtontimes.com/news/2017/mar/17/mayo-clinic-faces-questions-after-ceo-comments-on-/
3 https://www.dpreview.com/forums/post/57493873

---

the majority of healthcare expenditures are for hospitals and physicians, not for third-party administrators.

The US spends about $3.8 trillion annually on health care. This is what $3.8 trillion looks like: $3,800,000,000,000. A better way to wrap your head around that number is to say its 3.8 million *million* dollars, which looks like this: $3,800,000 million.

Breakdown of US Healthcare Spending (2011)

Prescriptions Drugs

As shown above, prescription drugs account for 10 percent of US healthcare expenditures.[4] Although 10 percent is not

4 https://en.wikipedia.org/wiki/Prescription_drug_prices_in_the_United_States#cite_note-JAMA2-2

a large piece of the pie, when the pie represents $3.8 trillion, 10 percent is still a large amount of money. Pharmaceuticals are an opportunity for savings.

The US pays more for prescription medicines than other countries because we do not have a national healthcare system with a single payer that is able to bargain and negotiate with the large, powerful pharmaceutical companies. One major advantage of a single-payer system is that it would help reduce our overall expenditure on drug prices. For instance, Canada, India, and the United Kingdom set price limits on the most commonly used drugs and generic medicines.

But we do not need a federal system in order to enact price control or to negotiate drug prices. Again, "single payer" does not have to mean a government-run national health system. The government could set a price maximum for every drug, if it wanted to, and then allow the private sector to bargain. Private payers already bargain with pharmaceutical companies.

As we allow the large, private healthcare plans like Kaiser Permanente and others to get larger, they will continue to consolidate. As they cover more patients, their ability to negotiate better prices will further reduce the overall costs. This consolidation reduces variability and administrative costs while it improves quality and increases the power of negotiating—one of the key ways to reduce the cost of drugs. This is another way in which insurance companies provide value that is often misunderstood.

It is often said that the US is the sole provider of the revenue that drug companies harvest to drive their research and development (R and D). R and D is a critical aspect of the pharmaceutics companies' process. And while it is critical to discover and develop new drugs, that development costs millions and millions of dollars.

Innovation in the pharmaceutical field is another key component in improving health care. We have to provide incentive for companies to be innovative. But few citizens understand the long, tedious, and expensive process of coming up with an innovative discovery or idea that actually helps patients. Innovations must make their way through the rigorous bench-work testing in a lab, through animal testing without any toxic sides effect, thought pharmacokinetics to identify the best dosing, and then through three phases of testing. It can take twenty years and cost more than 100 million dollars before a new medication makes its way through the FDA and finally onto the US market.

Some believe that pharmaceutical companies need to spend at least 10 percent of their gross revenue in R and D. While all of these facts are true, it is neither fair nor equitable that the US pays R and D costs for the whole world. All countries should share an equal burden for developing pharmaceuticals. The cost could be prorated on each country's usage, population, costs, and value.

The Fallacy of the Single Payer Argument

We often hear the argument that a single-payer system would be much cheaper than private insurance. As shown above, 7 percent of US health care dollars are spent on administrative costs—again, it's not a large percentage, but 7 percent of $3.8 trillion is a huge number. And our administrative cost is much higher than that of other countries. There is much opportunity here to reduce cost.

First, it is a misnomer to say that the United States does not have a single payer. In some sectors, we do. If you are poor, you have Medicaid—and that is a single payer. If you are older than sixty-five, you have Medicare—which is also a single payer. If you are a veteran of the United States armed forces, you have the VA—another single payer.

Moreover, as described above, the mistake is that people think the single payer has to be a government-run system. "Single payer" does not mean socialism or socialized medicine. Perhaps our best solution *is* a single payer, or two or three private payers that are not government-run, but we use the government to help regulate prices as well as negotiate costs.

The Sunday morning talk shows often incorrectly espouse the benefits of the single-payer systems in Europe that offer lower cost and better care at greater value than the US. But these statements are false, made by politicians who have never cared for a patient. Many have never lived or worked in Europe, and they haven't spent hours in an operating room like I have. They haven't had long meetings with the doctors and administrators in European or Asian or Australian Hospitals and clinics. I often hear that the European Countries have socialism and have "a single payer" that provides better care at lower prices. This is simply wrong.

Europe has a wide array of private insurance-type payers sprinkled in with socialist programs. It is true that there are some countries—such as Britain, Italy and Sweden, for example—where every citizen is enrolled in healthcare system that is not just government-paid, but government-run. This means there is universal health care for of the citizens and the doctors and nurses work for the government. This is the most extreme example of a single payer and is most correctly called socialized medicine. If you talk to the patients and doctors in that country, they'll tell you their healthcare system has many problems that should be obvious to all readers in a non-incentivized system.

In contrast, there are countries like our northern neighbor, Canada, where there is universal healthcare mandate. Health services are provided by the government, but physicians are mostly private and citizens often purchase additional private insurance. France has a similar system in some ways.

In the Netherlands, where I recently was, the insurance is provided by private companies—but universal coverage is mandatory, in the same way car insurance is mandatory in the US. This drives down the cost of premiums, as we have reiterated many times in this book. The government provides money to help pay for healthcare insurance, but is not the main provider. This system is one we find the most attractive for the US in its current state.

To those reading carefully, the Netherlands system should sound like Obama Care—and in fact, it is similar. But would a governmental single payer—something much different than a private single-payer system—be cheaper than private insurance? Does that idea even make sense? Can you think of anything in your own experience in which the government ran a process leaner, better, and more efficiently, with better customer service, than a similar process in the private sector?

Forget what people tell you and what you hear or read. Just think of your own, real-life experiences. Think about the mail, or consider the customer service you experience when it is time to renew your driver's license. Would government-run health care be any different?

Recently, Nevada has proposed that every person in the state should buy Medicaid. This is an inexpensive, single-payer, government-run system, and its advantages and disadvantages have been debated extensively. Fortunately for hospitals, the Republican governor of Nevada rejected the idea. Hospitals lose money on Medicaid patients because Medicaid reimbursement is so low. If you own a business, do you want to have more customers who lose you money? This is the business model that Medicaid patients represent to doctors and hospitals. The reimbursement of Medicaid patients would have to increase and enough taxes would have to be collected for a government-run system to be profitable.

Our Recommendation

In this arena, we make a clear recommendation for a solution. The US citizens, our physicians, and the insurance companies will not adopt a single, government-run payer, so that option is not feasible—nor is it attractive. However, a mixed system is.

We suggest the elimination of Medicaid. Because hospitals and physicians lose money on Medicaid patients, the system is not sustainable. Even worse, Medicaid tags or labels patients negatively while they are in the hospital. We believe those who are currently on Medicaid are enrolled. We believe Medicaid should be immediately dissolved and, as we discuss later in this book, the VA system should be slowly phased out (and we fully understand the political fallout and of that simple sentence).

The culture in those institutions is beyond repair. Our veterans deserve the best. Without the VA, they would have the choice of any private facility they wanted, and it would be paid by the US government—just not *delivered* by government. We have proven again and again that the current system does not work. The same could occur with The Indian Health System, allowing those enrolled to choose any hospital they want.

The current funding for Medicaid is transferred to each state's Medicare system. Children of uninsured parents are covered by Medicare through the CHIPS (Children Health Insurance Program) program. How do we pay for it? The money is part of the tax burden we pay in this country. But we need to reduce the cost of delivering these services. The private sector will, but the government will not. In fact, like the Netherlands, we should mandate coverage for everyone—but give them a choice.

Universal coverage for all US citizens is a fundamental belief of mine and a guiding principle of this book. I believe that coverage should be paid for by the government but NOT delivered by the government. The leanest healthcare delivery systems, which offer the best value, should earn more because more patients choose them. Giving patients a choice will drive innovation and improve quality by reducing cost. The truth is, we already do this with Medicare Advantage, although most people don't understand. We will outline it below. The government makes it convoluted, but we will try to explain it simply.

Medicare has Part A, which covers patients if and they are admitted into a hospital, and Part B, which pays for outpatient services such as clinic visits to your doctor. Medicare Part C is called the Medicare Advantage Plan; it involves additional coverage offered by private insurance companies, which make money by selling these policies. If you opt into Medicare Part C, you still have the Medicare Parts A and B, but the additional policy offers some additional advantages (such as easier referrals, better deals on your co-pay, etc.). These insurance providers take their premium from the money that the government would pay you monthly, and they are happy they get guaranteed money each month.

This is the kind of system we recommend. The government would provide the states the money that they already collect—no more—and allow each state to individualize its own system to fill in the gaps. This would lead to innovation and competition. Insurance companies would compete to provide the best product to patients, using the government's money. They would be happy, because they'd get guaranteed government money monthly, in addition to the extra policy premiums from the individuals they wrote to their plan. This system relies on capitalism because it creates competition—but it also uses federal money that has already been put aside for health care, and uses it in a much more valuable way with less cost.

Such a system also ensures that everyone has health insurance, which drives premiums down because it mandates the young and healthy to be involved either in a private insurance plan or through Medicare, which now is not restricted to citizens age sixty-five and older. It's a win-win situation. Finally, because one can never be sure if the money will truly be enough, we recommend a National Medicare Donation Program through which wealthy Americans who have private insurance willingly agree to donate back part or all of their Medicare money that has been withheld from their checks over the past forty years, to be used to subsidize deserving but poor Americans. These donations could be made publicly, to ensure the individuals generous enough to do this receive their due recognition.

Reducing Administrative Costs

One metric used to measure administrative costs is called the "payer's efficiency." It is calculated in part by this formula:

Payer's efficiency = Money spent on administrative costs / total costs of health care.

I have consulted for private insurers who are irritated and disappointed when newspapers or websites give Medicare a better efficiency score than insurance companies. Let's examine some of the reasons why news sites make this claim. Remember, data is only as good as the method used to collect it and the way the metrics are defined.

Medicare patients are all, by definition, sixty-five or older, while private insurance patients are generally younger. Medicare patients, therefore, have more co-morbidities (other health problems) and are likely to become ill with more complex medical conditions. Medicare patients, therefore, have a higher cost-per-patient.

This fact, by itself, artificially improves the metric in favor of the single payer, Medicare. When this metric is defined differently—for example, as cost per patient/ per severity of illness, instead of total cost—Medicare scores worse than private payers.

In addition, private payers like Community Health Systems (CHS) and HCA have to pay for software and even collection agencies to collect the money they are owed. Medicare has funds collected by other branches of the US government, which gives Medicare the benefit of 100 percent compliance and up-front payment of premiums; premiums are just pulled out of every paycheck we get, so the cost of collecting the premium is not included in the Medicare administrative costs. This artificially improves its efficiency metric again.

Furthermore, Medicare is deducted directly from US citizens without a state surcharge, whereas many states charge a 1.3 to 2.8 percent tax on private insurance companies. This state tax is added as an "administrative cost" to the private payers, which makes private payers look less efficient than Medicare.

All of these factors and others have led some news reports to falsely claim that the government is "leaner" than the private sector in administrating healthcare costs. I call this one of the many fallacies of the single payer.[5] A single payer that is not a single GOVERNMENT payer may have appeal.

A current example of the value in not having a single government payer system in the US can be seen in the Charlie Gard case that recently received worldwide attention. Charlie Gard was born in London with a rare disease with no known cure. His parents requested to take Charlie to the US for an experimental treatment.[6] The British doctors, the British Supreme Court, and the European Court on Human Rights denied them this opportunity.

Is there a single American reading this book that can imagine a hospital telling us that we cannot legally move our loved one from one hospital to another to improve their care, or that we cannot fire a doctor to find another one we like or trust more? We have the right to do this, and we exercise that right all the time. But we do not have a single-payer system.

---

5 http://thehill.com/blogs/pundits-blog/healthcare/337826-single-payer-healthcare-is-far-more-expensive-than-advocates

6 http://www.washingtonexaminer.com/the-lesson-everyone-missed-in-the-charlie-gard-story/article/2630800

We have the freedom of choice because US healthcare does not have that level of government involvement.

Perhaps, if Charlie's parents had been American, they would have been able to take their child abroad for treatment sooner. The outcome might not have been different, but having a choice might have decreased the indescribable agony of watching a critically ill newborn baby dying before their eyes.

There is value in insurance companies. Americans think they only make big profits for the CEOs, but this is not true. There is value in avoiding the single-payer system in favor of a system that creates competition and encourages novel ways to provide better care at lower cost. Monopolies are frowned upon in all other business sectors. Why would health care be different?

As noted previously, the mere fact that insurance companies are making a profit does not mean they are not valuable for patients, as well as for hospitals and physicians. However, nearly every practicing physician will tell you that insurance paperwork and regulations have stripped away the physician's engagement in patient care and sapped the physician's desire to go to work every day. We spend more time on paperwork and forms then we spend seeing and caring for our patients. We spend additional hours on hold, day after day, waiting for a peer-to-peer phone approval to get a test that a patient so obviously needs. These processes must be streamlined and standardized.

Private insurance is not going to go away. For-profit operators of healthcare facilities, like Hospital Corporation of America (HCA), are here to stay. HCA has 243,000 employees and 56,000 doctors, and they own 211 hospitals. They provide many Americans with quality jobs (and health insurance) and produce outstanding outcomes for patients by using metrics and information in ways that motivate providers to improve the quality of care they deliver at lower costs.

I currently work at New York Langone Medical Center, which is one of the eight top-ranked hospitals in the United States. Langone achieved this honor by measuring doctors and nurses in many ways and driving their behavior in order to achieve the best outcomes possible for patients.

NYU Langone has created an entire culture of excellence—but you can only improve what you measure. Physicians, nurses, and administrators at Langone own their outcomes and are taught not to complain about the metrics chosen or the way in which they are scored—even though the metrics and dashboards are always changing, and the bar gets higher every day as the metrics implemented become better aligned. This is what high-performing organizations and teams do.

The truth is that the insurance agencies ensure a higher quality of care than government-funded health care provides. Private insurers are currently able to do it better than the government programs. If we prevent private insurers like HCA—or academic healthcare centers like NYU Langone— from making a profit, what happens to all the people they employ and all the hospitals they operate? What happens to the patients they care for? Trying to make such drastic changes would lead to high unemployment and lower quality health care.

Insurance companies, hospitals, and physicians are all in it to make as much money as possible. Like any good business, they realize the best way to do that is to provide the best product for the lowest cost with the highest patient satisfaction. And that's okay. We just need to get aligned so that all stakeholders have an incentive to provide the highest quality of care at the lowest cost.

When the highest profits are made because we are offering the best care, we are becoming aligned. When patients, physicians, hospitals, and insurance companies ask, "What does that test or operation cost, and is it necessary?"—because both patients *and* insurance companies have to pay for part of it—then we are aligned. But few patients ever ask me the cost of a test that I order prior to doing their lung resection for lung cancer.

A step in the right direction would be to set up a system that ensures that hospitals and physicians are paid based upon the number of lives saved and the number of patients who experience an improved quality of life, instead of the number of procedures performed or patients seen. This would emphasize *quality* of care over *volume* of care—although how quality is defined is another question.

The truth is that today, volume still trumps quality, since the latter is still too subjectively measured and is often assessed through a myopic lens of thirty- and ninety-day metrics.

The Insurance Dilemma

Insurance companies were happy when Obama Care was passed. Healthcare stocks soared, because many hospitals that care for indigent and uninsured patients have lost millions of dollars on those patients.

Like most physicians, I see *everyone* in my clinic: the rich and the poor, the indigent and the VIP, the mansion-dweller and the homeless. However, I just give my time. The hospital has more to lose.

When I see an uninsured patient and perform a robotic lobectomy for lung cancer, and they spend two to three days in the hospital, the hospital loses thousands of dollars. Doctors do this all the time. Most of us have been caring for the uninsured for years.

But the hospitals cannot afford to do this anymore. To stay open, they have to make enough profit on the insured patients to pay for the patients who will never be able to pay.

Obama Care meant that everyone would have to have at least *some* insurance.

Why Obama Care Failed

The way Obama Care was supposed to work was to mandate that all citizens—every person in the USA—was insured. This is a good idea, in my opinion, and the right thing to do. This means that many young people—most of whom are healthy and unlikely to require admission to the hospital—would have to pay into the system now.

This is how insurance companies make money, but also how they keep the risk and the price down. They are experts at assessing the risk of someone dying, getting cancer, being admitted to the hospital, etc. They spread the risk over more people, including those who almost certainly won't need medical care, which lowers the cost for the small percentage who are going to need medical care.

So why has Obama Care failed? The political uncertainty under the Trump administration has put insurance companies in an unworkable position. They've had to contend with the threat of the individual mandate being repealed—which would mean that only individuals who really needed medical care would have insurance. The companies would have to set higher prices for those individuals, because the risk would no longer be spread over a large group.

The Trump administration has been unclear about whether there will be federal dollars placed aside to subsidize some of these initiatives. Some insurance companies have abandoned their offers, pulling out of the exchanges because they couldn't determine whether there would be any money available for the insured to pay their premiums. This has furthered hastened the death of Obama Care, as more and more insurance companies have had to back out because of potentially huge financial losses.

Another nail in the coffin has been the fact that a few of the promises of Obama Care have not been kept. Although it might have been Obama's honest intention to let all patients keep their health plans and their doctors, because of the Affordable Care Act's construction, that proved not to be possible. Critics of Obama Care have been able to point out that a cornerstone promise of that plan was not kept.

Because of all these factors, premiums have gone up for many Americans since Obama Care was initiated. The average citizen with a higher premium is likely to blame Obama Care rather than the uncertainty of the federal government's support for the plan.

One of the cornerstones of our solution is lower premiums on the youngest and most healthy people in the US, who are not in a position to subsidize the oldest and sickest Americans. Young people are just starting their adult lives and not yet earning much money. Many are already in debt from their educations.

We suggest a simple solution based on the principle that all US citizens must have insurance: every adult and every child. Focusing on that goal aligns several stakeholders, as described above. More importantly, taking care of our citizens is the right thing to do.

Caring and loving societies take care of their sick, their poor, and their under-privileged. We do not have to actively seek them out, but we must take care of those that are ours. This is who I am, and it is who The United States of America is and always has been.

The long-term solution is preventive care and population health.

Population Health

Population health is a poorly understood term. It can mean many things, but most experts agree it is a way to for an organized healthcare system to improve the health of its members.

By pure definition population health means health outcomes—which can represent a large, diverse number of metrics—of a defined group of individuals. The members could be the entire citizen population of the USA, or it might be a sub-group, such as a group of teachers. The bigger the group, the more impact the solution will have—but of course, the larger the group, the more heterogeneous the population becomes.

Population health might be most effective if divided into homogenous groups of patients with similar cultures and risk factors. A program for health can measure each patient's risk and the effectiveness of a type of preventive care or the efficacy of a specific intervention. This science will eventually provide data on ways to spend less to deliver more health and a better quality of life. It will not necessarily include doctor's care, but it will make better health and greater patient choice available to large groups of people.

Patient Choice

We see that the healthcare industry is a business, and that it needs improvement. The question is, how do we slowly phase out aspects of our healthcare system that are no longer serving us? I believe the best way to do this is to give more power to the patients and allow them to make their own choices.

As I have described, in my view, health care is a right; *everyone* should have access to health care. But I also believe private businesses should have the right to deny or charge more for services to people who make bad choices like smoking, drinking, overeating, or otherwise failing to take care of themselves. When people make choices that endanger their health, they should still be able to receive care, of course—but at an increased cost. Others will argue that people who make poor health choices should only have access to government-funded care, through a system similar to the VA hospital system or Medicaid.

The significance of this model is that people are able to exercise their right to choose, but just like in other aspects of their life, poor decisions must have consequences. Yet everyone has access to at least a minimal level of care.

We can and should let patients decide whether they want private insurance or government care. If the government offers a good plan, they'll pick it. If the government provides patients with outstanding hospitals and low premiums, then everyone will opt for government-funded care. Currently, patients are not given a choice. Medicare premiums are taken out of your paycheck, and you are forced to participate at the age of sixty-five, whether you want to or not.

In addition, if patients want extra dental care or vision care or a concierge service—let them pay for it. We can give patients the choice with the corresponding cost, just as we do in most every other sector in life. The difference is, in this sector, we must provide high-quality service to everyone as a bare minimum.

The key is *choice*. Lack of choice is an impediment to improving our current healthcare system. The Veterans Affairs (VA) Department is a great example. Veterans who have incurred life-altering physical or mental injuries in the course of defending our country are often forced to receive their treatment at VA hospitals. I believe our vets should be able to get care anywhere they want to go, and the government should pay.

One centerpiece solution offered in this book is this point. Let our veterans—our national heroes—choose where they want to get medical care. We are aware that some plans already allow for this. If vets were allowed to receive care from their providers of choice, it would greatly reduce the money the federal government spends on VA hospitals. In fact, many VA hospitals would be forced to close, because they currently provide a lower quality of care than hospitals in the private sector.

VA hospitals have been immune to efforts to change their culture or behavior because their customers have no choice but to come to them. Our nation's best, our vets, should have the option to choose their care at any hospital they want. Let's pay for them to go where they want to go. If the well-run VA facilities—and there are many—continue to improve their patient care, then they will survive. By changing their culture and standards, they will be able to compete with their local private-sector hospitals.

Some might argue that we can't afford to send everyone to private insurance, and that VA care is more cost-effective. In fact, the opposite is true. VA health care is not a competitive, patient-centered, or cost-effective system. A lot of resources go to providing VA employees with extra paid time off, early retirement, sick days, and other benefits that private insurers and other hospitals just cannot afford to offer.

People who work at a VA facility and are reading this may disagree. I know many incredibly hard-working and great VA employees—but facts are facts. I'm not some politician who has walked through a few VA hospitals while campaigning. I have worked in a VA hospital for many years. The fixed operating costs of most VA hospitals cost the government more money than would have been spent just sending veterans to more efficient facilities.

We are aware many will argue this point. My response is, give the customer the option. Let him or her go wherever they want to go, and let's see what they decide.

Many VA healthcare facilities occupy valuable real estate. If we eliminate VA health care, these VA buildings could function as rehabilitation centers or nursing homes, or provide other aspects of desperately needed care besides tertiary acute care. If they don't provide enough value in that way, the government could sell the buildings and put that money toward paying for veterans' health care or paying down the deferral deficit.

These statements will infuriate many readers who work in VA hospitals and have dedicated their lives to the VA system. I agree that many VA facilities are high-quality hospitals that offer great care—but we have to be truthful in order to solve the healthcare crisis. Despite the millions of great people who provide our vets with love and care, the nation's healthcare system—including the VA—is broken.

Lower Premiums

One reason the Obama Care has failed is that people's premiums have gone up. The Obama Care idea was a good one. Everyone was mandated to get health care, so young and healthy people would have to pay into the system, which would drive down the overall cost.

But the vast majority of young, heathy people in the US have debt from college. They are just getting married or might have young children at home. They cannot afford any premiums—not even modest ones—especially for a benefit they will almost never use. So why should we insist they pay for it unless we can offer lower premiums?

One solution to our healthcare crisis has to be to deliver much lower premiums than we have today for these healthy, young patients. And remember, this is by far the largest percent of Americans we have to serve. Only 10 percent of patients are elderly, ill, and poor, but they consume 80 percent of the US healthcare dollars.

How can we make it affordable for healthy people to share some of this cost burden?

We can offer a lot of options. The first one is to eliminate the high-risk patients who use 80 percent of the healthcare dollars from this pool. Auto insurance companies do this:

drivers pay different rates based on the risk they present to the company. It is well-known that a small percentage of the US population is responsible for at least 50 percent of overall healthcare costs.[7]

We can care for high-risk patients, who require special attention, in a different system. Their healthcare costs can be addressed directly by our federal tax dollars—not by charging higher premiums for millions of young, healthy patients who do not use the system. Care for the most expensive, sickest patients can be paid for with the billions of dollars already taken out of the paychecks of our wealthiest Americans.

Most states have funds that could be set aside with much lower administrative costs and used directly to pay for these high-risk patients, many of whom have pre-existing conditions and are indigent. These patients are what our taxes are for. Each state should govern this independently and pay a penalty if they are not fiscally neutral in covering *all* of their citizens' healthcare costs.

Health Savings Accounts

While we discuss Health Savings Accounts (HSAs) in depth in Chapter 10, it is an important topic here because these accounts present a great opportunity to increase patient choice. HSAs allow us to set aside a fixed percentage of our

7 https://www.theatlantic.com/business/archive/2012/01/5-of-americans-made-up-50-of-us-health-care-spending/251402/

paychecks, before taxes are taken out, and use those funds for healthcare expenses.

People are more likely to spend their money wisely when it is pulled directly from their paychecks—and there is 20 to 40 percent more of it, because it has not been taxed. If a patient is paying for a MRI out of his or her HSA, they're not likely to get the scan that costs $2,500 when the same service is being offered for $2,100 down the street. If you have a nodule in your breast and the doctor suggests that an MRI might be helpful, you and your doctor will need to decide together whether one is needed (it might not be). You might decide on the far less expensive option of an ultrasound or a CT scan. These types of protocols, written by medical experts and implemented by some insurance companies, will become a greater part of the fabric and framework of our solution.

When the cost is being paid out of their own health savings accounts, patients will begin questioning the efficiency, cost, and necessity of all recommended tests and treatments. This is a cornerstone of our offered healthcare solution.

I've practiced medicine for more than twenty-five years, and I have never had a patient ask me what a PET scan costs, although I've ordered thousands of them. When MDs are responsible for their cost of care and have to own their outcomes as well as their costs, which will be publically displayed, patients will do the same.

Of course, many people are hesitant to enact this type of change because most patients are not educated enough about the complexities of health care to understand what procedures are necessary and what they should cost. It will become our job, as healthcare providers, to educate patients and truthfully tell them whether they actually need a MRI for this breast mass or whether a chest CT or mammogram and ultrasound would be adequate.

Doctors should be able to offer patients a list of options so that they can make informed decisions together. National protocols for every conceivable type of health problem are being written and can be used to guide—not mandate— healthcare decisions.

Healthcare providers have created protocols for the best and least expensive options for every possible situation. In fact, this is already happening for various cancers through the NCCN[8] Guidelines, and we can expand these guidelines to cover every specialty, illness, injury, and disease. We can set up protocols for almost every problem and recommend the most efficient, effective, and cheapest method of treatment for most of our patients. We can include what the possible treatments or tests cost at each hospital and what type of care is offered at each hospital.

We will get to the point that the patient won't even have to ask, "Do I need this test?" because the answer will be published and ready for them online, and they can look it up prior to their visit with us. Once patients are empowered to ask these

---

8 NCNN—the National Comprehensive Cancer Network, an alliance of twenty-seven cancer centers throughout the United States, most of which are designated by the National Cancer Institute (one of the US National Institutes of Health) as comprehensive cancer centers.

questions, they will have a much greater investment in the care they receive, and this will drive healthcare costs down.

Finally, HSAs are currently only available to people who have high-deductible health plans. This regulatory rule needs to be changed. HSAs should be available to all Americans who work, just like IRA or 457 plans are.

Physician Independence

Physicians are also frustrated by the various impediments to improving our healthcare system. Physicians hate to be managed—generally, their attitude is, *I didn't go to school until I was thirty-two just to have to call an insurance company to get a test approved by someone with no medical training who is blindly reading a script.* Yet this is the process that most physicians who see insured patients have to follow.

Redundant and unnecessary testing is another problem. Physicians often feel compelled to order every test possible because they're afraid of being sued, but insurance companies want to pay for as few tests as possible.

If we were to generate a standard-of-care protocol with very specific criteria for how we're going to manage a lung nodule, for example—and if we mandated that adherence to this protocol would protect the doctor from the possibility of a lawsuit—then lawsuits would decrease, and many insurance company approvals wouldn't be necessary.

The implementation of national guidelines would serve to greatly reduce healthcare costs while making delivery more efficient. It would also affect the other costly part of this equation—physicians practicing defensive medicine prompted by fear of lawsuits.

But in order for this to work, we must align lawyers in this process as well—and our current system is far away from this.

In Conclusion

Moving our healthcare system to a more capitalist model—rather than to a socialist one—will be beneficial. We need providers and patients alike to have a high level of investment in the system. We need to be able to provide everyone with access to health care, while also taking a more comprehensive approach to educating patients and taking socioeconomic factors into account.

Our healthcare system can change, but we must work together toward the change we need. Every single person reading this book is more empowered than they may realize.

Many avenues have been established to give you the opportunity to share your experience and to express your frustrations. Your voice *does* matter. The more you get your story out there, the better the strengths and weaknesses of our current system will be understood by legislators, lobbyists, and the people who sit on the boards of insurance companies and other entities that comprise our healthcare system.

We want people to be more informed when they are in a position to effect change and to make informed decisions about their health care.

Chapter 3

THE SOLUTION BEGINS
WITH ALIGNMENT

W HEN IT COMES TO HEALTH CARE, ALL OF THE
four major stakeholders—insurance companies, physicians,
hospitals, and patients—seem to have different agendas. This
lack of alignment is a major contributor to the problems in
our healthcare system.

Patients are, in fact, stakeholders in the process, although
they generally do not engage with their own health care
on this level. In order to improve our healthcare system,
patients must take on more accountability and understand
their role as stakeholders in their own health. Although we
firmly believe that all patients should have access to high-
quality health care, we must acknowledge that the patient
has responsibilities as well.

Each of the stakeholders in a health care system must be aligned concerning the purpose of health care so that we can create an effective and efficient national healthcare system. How do we get all these stakeholders aligned? The solutions are tied to the problems.

Physicians are paid for procedures, so the more procedures we perform, the more we get paid. In this way, we actually have an incentive for the patient to do poorly. If a patient has a surgery and then experiences complications and we have to operate on them again, we get paid more. Or at least, this is how the system used to work.

Some hospitals also are paid for each day that a patient is in the hospital, which is an incentive for them to keep people longer—but longer hospital stays ultimately delay recovery and take up needed hospital beds. Other hospitals are given a set amount of money based on a patient's admission diagnosis code, so their incentive is to send patients home as soon as possible.

This is not to insinuate that physicians and hospitals are intentionally impeding patient recovery. However, we are likely to see great improvements in our healthcare system if we incentivize lives saved and improved quality of life rather than procedures performed and days kept in the hospital. We have seen a trend toward quality of care and not volume of care, and this trend needs to continue.

To further complicate matters, most patients don't have an incentive to quickly recover and return home, either. The ideal situation would be to have patients come to physicians and hospitals in relatively good shape and then leave healthy and able to care for themselves. In reality, however, many patients *want* to spend extra days in the hospital.

These patients are admitted in poor condition because they have not taken care of themselves—they do not work out and exercise several days a week and they have unhealthy habits. If the patient doesn't have someone to care for him or her at home, they want to stay in the hospital, where they are attended to throughout the day.

Additionally, patients are not paying for the procedures they undergo, so they generally don't know what their care costs. They also don't question the quality of care they are receiving. As noted in the previous chapter, people are less engaged in the service they are receiving when they are not paying for it.

Of course, most people care about the quality of care they receive, but they usually don't look into it beyond asking family or friends for recommendations. Patients do not have enough information to know whether they are following the best, most cost-effective treatment plan. And despite myriad online rankings of MDs and hospitals, the data is difficult to understand. We are data rich but information poor.

Some patients are not disposed toward long-term health planning and healing, any more than the physicians and hospitals are, because they don't understand medical procedures or costs and don't feel empowered to evaluate their own quality of care. They also might feel they are unable to afford a healthier lifestyle.

Most insurance companies now reduce payments to hospitals each day that the patient is still in the hospital. For example, on the first day, the hospital may receive $800; the next day it will receive $600, and so on. This encourages hospitals to discharge patients who are doing well and to bring in new patients as soon as possible.

Most large hospitals in the United States run at 85 percent occupancy or higher, which indicates that one of the biggest problems for hospitals is getting patients through the system quickly enough. If we can change how insurance companies pay hospitals, it will make a big difference in getting patients better more quickly.

More and more hospitals have taken on *throughput*[1] *projects* to get patients into and then out of the hospital more quickly, since building new hospital beds is very expensive and often not financially possible.

During my time at University at Alabama in Birmingham (UAB), I was the Chair of the Business Intelligence team. We spearheaded a project to help the hospital with their throughput level for operating rooms.

The board that governs hospital operations raised concerns that the 1,200-bed hospital was running at 90 percent occupancy rate. They wanted to build another two hundred beds, which would have cost the hospital about $500 million. This

---

1 *Throughput* is the term hospitals use to describe the number of people who go through their system.

was just not financially feasible. Our suggestion was that, rather than adding beds, we should reduce our length of stay—increase our *throughput*—by treating the hospital as if it had a capacity of 1,300 beds.

Reducing our overall length of stay just from 6.7 days to 6.2 days had the same effect as adding about sixty beds. We spent a few months figuring out what bottleneck was causing the delay in patient discharge. Once we found the problem, the solution was extremely simple.

It turned out that a major problem was that the doctors weren't writing discharge orders for patients until about noon, which meant that patient continued to spend the entire day of their discharge in the hospital. The patients then had to be given lunch, and nurses had to delay giving patients their exit instructions until later in the day.

We were able to change this by explaining the problems to the doctors. We then generated scorecards on what percent of their patients had a "discharge home" order by nine a.m., and we shared their scores publically. Most people are inherently competitive, and doctors are especially so. We capitalized on this fact and quickly drove scores up.

With more patients having their discharge orders in hand by nine a.m., beds were freed up earlier in the day, which allowed new patients from the recovery room and the emergency room to go directly into their hospital beds. We continued to publically display how the MDs were doing compared to their peers in writing the orders before nine a.m. because we had discovered that this data drove their behavior, which aligned with the hospital's goal of a shorter average length of stay.

The drive for earlier discharge orders also aligned with the patients' desires to go home early in morning. They wanted to avoid traffic and get back into their own homes. Finally, it aligned with the insurance companies' desire to spend less money. This is just one example of how novel approaches can align teammates.

This situation also shows the importance of giving patients an incentive to leave the hospital. If the patient were charged more for staying in the hospital longer, this would change their behavior.

The cost of one day on the floor, at most US hospitals, is about $900. So if patients want to stay in the hospital longer—even though they are eating, all catheters are out, and there's no medical reason to keep them—they should have to pay a percentage of that cost. This would further align stakeholders and motivate patients to advocate for themselves to ensure that they are not paying out-of-pocket for inpatient care they no longer need.

Cost and Value

All of the stakeholders *seem* to have different agendas, but in reality, the desired outcome for each is for patients to have the highest quality of care at the lowest cost. The key here is *cost*, which tends to be left out of conversations about improving our healthcare system. Remember that:

Value = Quality/Cost

Applying a little basic mathematics to this, we can also calculate that cost is quality divided by value. In order to understand cost, we must first look at value. Essentially, if you have really high quality and really low cost, that's great value.

Lowering Cost

This is the lowest-hanging fruit. It is by far the easiest way to improve value and one that does not take much imagination. However, its implementation has been incredibly poor. Hospitals have overcharged for routine patient care over the past twenty years, and the amount of waste has been and still is staggering. If the average business owner came to the hospital and saw the amount of wasted raw material and process, he would be shocked. Profit margins for hospitals were so high, no one really seemed to care that we wasted a few hundred dollars during most every operation or encounter. The myopic surgeon did not care because it was "not his money"—it was the hospital's. Now the more enlightened surgeon realizes that the hospital is the doctor and the doctor is the hospital. We are one.

The Physician = The Hospital

This is true whether you are in private practice or academic medicine, or if you send your patients to more than one hospital for their care. Regardless of the financial relationship between physicians and healthcare facilities, we cannot take good care of our patients without proper resources, and resources cost money. Physicians—especially surgeons—want all of their expensive toys, and operating room nurses try hard to have all of the equipment there just in case we need it. But this can lead to huge excess.

There are thousands of ways we can lower costs while maintaining, if not improving, quality. I have written articles on this, and many others are working on other novel and interesting ideas. A recent example can be seen by a project we did at UAB. One operation we commonly performed requires about five to six surgical instruments. My partners also perform the same operation frequently, about two to three times a week, and they may use a few more instruments—but not many. However, when the surgical trays came to my operating room, there were more than seventy surgical instruments on them. There was one I did not even recognize, so I asked the most senior nurse what it was. She said a surgeon that had retired from the hospital about twenty-two years earlier had wanted it "just in case," but he had never used it.

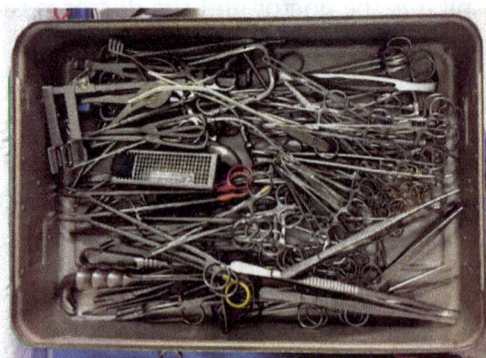

Before

The instrument in question is circled above. It looks more like an egg beater to me then a delicate, precise surgical instrument. Yet that instrument, along with the other seventy instruments, had been washed, clean, wrapped, counted and sterilized thousands of times over the past twenty years. Even worse, many of the instruments—including the egg beater—had been repurchased, since they were on the tray and were assumed to be "necessary." Despite the fact that these instruments were not being used, their maintenance created a significant cost for the hospital. We proposed a plan of eliminating fifty-three such instruments, and we were met with agreement across the board. The surgical tray now looks like this:

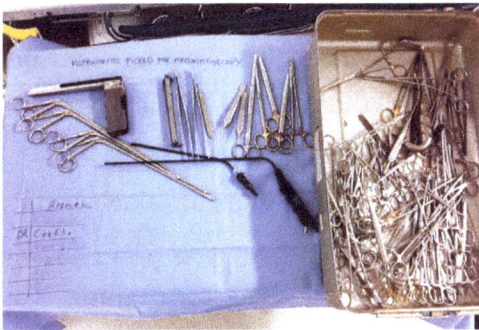

After

This is one example of lowering costs without affecting quality, which in turn increases value. It also makes the nurse's job easier; they have lighter trays to carry and fewer instruments to count before and after each operation, which saves operating room time. One minute in most operating rooms costs between

$300 and $500 dollars—yes, each *minute*, because of the operating cost and the personnel that are present and required.

There are hundreds of other projects that we, and other healthcare providers, are doing as well. Any physician reading this book should pretend that they are paying personally for everything they see around them in the hospital or clinic where they work. I'm betting that, within a few minutes, they can think of several ways to reduce costs. The key is to engage the entire team to think this way and then to actually implement some of their ideas.

If a patient needs a lung operation, how would we measure *value* in this situation? Most surgeons will talk about some of the metrics that we view as surrogates for quality: for example, they would mention minimizing blood loss, getting all the cancer out, and removing necessary lymph nodes. They might include some more subjective details as well, such as minimal patient pain and the return to a high quality of life within two weeks.

While these are all indicators of value when it comes to a lung operation, they are shortsighted. Real value is a long-term prospect. When you buy a car, for example, you want the highest quality at the lowest cost—but you wouldn't ask how the car will run in two weeks after purchase or even ninety days. You would ask how the car will perform in five years, seven years, and ten years.

If we expect a car to last eight years, we should expect a surgery to last at least that long (depending on the reason why it is performed, of course). I believe cancer operations *should* be measured in this way, with metrics for stage-specific survival rates, the number of re-interventions for recurrences, and quality of life. But currently, cancer surgeries are not evaluated in this way.

Quality is tied to the desired outcome and includes the length of the hospital stay. But judging quality becomes more complicated when we take into account the care of patients with chronic diseases like diabetes or hypertension. Chronic disease does not have an admission date, operation date, and discharge date; instead, there is the date of diagnosis, followed by care that extends through the end of the patient's life.

What, then, does quality of care mean for chronically ill patients? How do we measure this over the span of twenty-five years? We would include how often the patient is hospitalized. For a diabetic patient, we should consider how well he controls his blood sugar level and whether he has developed consequences of the disease, like kidney problems, limb infections, or vision deterioration. But every MD will tell you this outcome may depend more on the patient's compliance with our medicines and diet than it does on the care we provide. If that's true, how can we give the MD a grade on caring for this chronically ill patient?

When we examine cost, value, and quality, it becomes obvious that cost and quality go hand-in-hand. If our shared vision is to provide quality care at the lowest cost, we must approach this vision with the understanding that we cannot achieve the lowest cost and neglect quality of care.

In general, as we provide higher quality care, our costs go down. Lower costs result from learning how to give better care. Once we have tweaked our protocols and made them leaner, our volume goes up, which allows us to purchase products we need to care for patients at a lower cost.

We need to agree, then, that providing high-quality care is the path to achieving the lowest cost.

Getting Aligned

Since our common goal is to provide quality care at the lowest cost, we need to ensure that all stakeholders are aligned with this goal. Any surgery has both a direct and an indirect cost. The direct cost is all the instruments we use: staplers, surgical equipment, sheets, bandages, and so forth. The indirect costs are the cost of doing business—for example, the number of nurses assisting with the surgery, the cost to heat and cool the operating room, the food we give the patient during his recovery stay, etc.

Given the many factors involved, the only way to get all the stakeholders aligned is to have an incredible degree of transparency when it comes to the actual costs of care. Transparency will go a long way toward aligning expectations among all stakeholders, including patients.

Patients who become educated and empowered will ask, "What is the cost of that test, and do I really need it?" When patients and doctors both start asking these questions routinely, because they both have skin in the game, we will know that our system is finally engaging all stakeholders. Patients will learn to ask the same kinds of questions they would ask when purchasing a car. Do you really need that high-end sound system? Well, what does it cost, and what is it worth to you?

The path to engaging patients on this level is complicated. The solution is *not* to eliminate insurance companies, because most people would not be able to afford health care on their own. But if patients paid for a portion of the care they received, they would have more investment in it. This model can be similar to auto insurance: the number of accidents you have directly affects your premium. In health care, the determining factors could be behavioral—smoking, obesity, and substance abuse, for example.

Health care is both a right *and* a privilege; everyone should have access to health care, but the cost should be determined by the patient's investment in his or her own health. A patient's behavior should determine, to some extent, what they pay.

Those with so-called "pre-existing conditions" are easy— we should take care of all such patients. But if you suffer from a condition caused by a poor *choice* you made—such as smoking—we will still take care of you, but your cost should be higher.

In order to ensure that the hospitals are aligned, we need to create incentives for them as well. Hospitals want patients who are insured, which means we should mandate coverage for all patients. First and most important, it is the right thing to do—the humane and caring thing to do. We are a caring nation. We should care for all US citizens, regardless of their economic status.

The economic reason for universal coverage is also clear. Healthcare stocks went up when Obama Care was passed because it meant more people had some type of insurance. For years, hospitals lost large sums of money on patients with no insurance. This national debate about whether everyone should have health care is somewhat moot—for years, we have been taking care of everyone anyway.

Since more and more physicians are employed by hospitals, what is beneficial for hospitals is also beneficial for physicians. This, in turn, is also beneficial for insurance companies. Universal health care actually serves to align hospitals and insurance companies.

Now insurance companies want to send patients to the hospitals with the lowest cost, and this aligns hospitals and physicians to empower patients to question cost and care—and that aligns us to provide higher quality care.

Readmissions—new hospital stays that happen soon after patients are discharged—are examples of costly, low-quality care. Insurance companies are making hospitals pay for readmissions. This has shifted the cost to the outpatient side, as MDs have devised novel ways to keep patients from being readmitted.

In order to align stakeholders on this, insurance companies can include in their hospital contracts that they won't cover readmission. If a patient has an operation and is readmitted thirty or ninety days after discharge, the hospital now has to cover *all* associated costs. If readmissions are simply not covered, hospitals and physicians will be incentivized to ensure quality care and follow-up that help deal with post-operative problems as outpatient care.

Healthcare providers will have an incentive to find ways to motivate patients to take better care of themselves at home, since most patients do not like readmission, either. Again, we need patients to have skin in this game. Some patients want to be readmitted because they do not have someone at home to tend to their needs. But those with adequate home care are likely to want to stay at home.

All stakeholders will be aligned to this shared goal if patients pay for part of their health care, since this will encourage them to shop around. If a hospital can offer lower costs or better quality care, patients are going to go there. In order to attract more patients, hospitals will strive to provide great customer service at a low cost. This translates to updated and clean facilities, great food, comfortable waiting rooms, and convenient parking—not just great doctors.

This is what alignment will look like: a win-win situation for everyone involved.

In Conclusion

This chapter has proposed possible solutions to the problems afflicting our healthcare system. These are not the final solutions, and that's okay.

The important first step is to have these conversations and better understand the forces that are currently pulling the teammates apart. The focus should be on developing a shared understanding that everyone can succeed together in providing the best health care at the lowest cost. We will devise a system in which quality is expected and provided. Value will be measured by long-term health and by improvements in behavior and self-care.

We are not all aligned financially right now, but paying hospitals and physicians for quality instead of quantity will be a step in the right direction, once we better define quality care. The first step toward achieving this is to discuss the concept with representatives of all the stakeholders.

Chapter 4

BIG DATA IS ONE KEY
TO SOLVING HEALTH CARE

THE POTENTIAL FOR DATA TO ASSIST IN HEALTH-
care cost reduction should not be overlooked. In fact, data
that is accurate and meaningful—not just lots of information,
but the right information—will be the key to solving the
healthcare crisis.

The term *big data* refers to all the information that is pulled
from millions and millions of patients, hospitals, physicians,
and surgeons. This data does not include patient names or
case studies, but just the numbers and how they relate to one
another. For instance, big data may include the number of
people within a specific age range who undergo a particular
procedure for a common type of cancer, and their survival
rates one or two or three years later.

In this chapter, we'll explore what big data means within the context of health care and how data can be transformative in terms of delivering quality care while reducing costs.

Big data is already generating powerful calculations that are shaping the future of health care. However, it is important to note that our data must be *accurate* if we are to use it to improve our quality of care while lowering costs. A data analyst in Canada has recently been promulgating data from which he draws the conclusion that cancer survival rates are higher in Sweden, Switzerland, Finland, and some African countries[1]—but is his data trustworthy?

Conclusions are tied to the accuracy of the data. In order to compare health care in different countries, we must ensure that patients are being diagnosed in the same way. In the US, more women receive screening mammograms and more men get PSA blood level tests to screen for prostate cancer than in many European countries. We now even offer lung cancer screening tests. Screening tests turn up more treatable cancers—but that can make cancer rates look higher.

The future of medicine involves a greater dependence on metrics to help make decisions and to track best practices for every procedure and treatment option—but many of the large administrative databases do not have the data needed, and much of what they do have is just incorrect.

---

1 http://www.cancerresearchuk.org/health-professional/cancer-statistics/ worldwide-cancer/mortality#collapseZero

Errors in the system have two primary causes. Procedures for collecting and entering data can lead to errors. But some people also are "gaming the system"—i.e., intentionally using the rules and processes of a system to manipulate the data and results.

In a *New York Times* article, Gary Marcus and Ernest Davis write, "Even when the results of a big data analysis aren't intentionally gamed, they often turn out to be less robust than they initially seem."[2] Data science is a booming field of research, but we have not yet developed the capability to identify inaccurate data.

Inaccurate big data is extremely problematic, and data that is not collected is equally troublesome. Conclusions drawn from data that is compared but does not share the same definition are not trustworthy. With all the information and correlations that big data provides, the gaps in the data hinder us from being able to distinguish the valid relationships between the data from those that are insignificant.

We cannot complete a data "puzzle" if too many pieces are missing. We must overcome several other hurdles before we can realize the full potential of medical big data.

National Databases

Accurate big data pulled from administrative, clinical, and financial databases will give us a powerful tool in helping

---

2 Gary Marcus and Ernest Davis, "Eight (No, Nine!) Problems with Big Data, *New York Times*, April 6, 2014 https://www.nytimes.com/2014/04/07/opinion/eight-no-nine-problems-with-big-data.html?_r=0

make decisions that serve to improve our healthcare system. Yet the countless databases currently used by hospitals, physicians, surgeons, medical researchers, and insurance companies do not communicate with one another. Medical conferences and other meetings of surgeons and physicians often feature reports pulled from national databases, but the majority of data is from administrative databases that provide details on patient demographics and diagnostic information—but not on patient treatment details. This is absurd. The treatment and the outcomes are what matter, especially for medical practitioners.

We cannot reach valuable conclusions or obtain insights from the relationships between the data until all of our databases are connected and communicate with each other. Databases also must and share the same definitions and must be checked for valid and accurate entry.

Financial databases used by hospitals contain a wealth of data on patient ages, residence zip codes, incomes, and amounts paid for health care received. But in most institutions, financial databases don't link well to the clinical databases, which document the patient's diagnosis, form of treatment, date treatment was stopped, and outcome. From a medical perspective, the relationship between the data from financial and clinical databases may prove extremely valuable—but we cannot know until they are synched.

Further, the information within our national databases is rarely, if ever, validated. Two years ago, a research report showed that US organizations believed 32 percent of their big data to be inaccurate.[3] The percentage may be much larger than that.

Physicians, nurses, and administrators input data based on interviews, documents, meetings, reports, and procedures—but there is no system in place to ensure that the information was entered correctly. We must establish systems for checking accuracy while also providing incentive for organizations to ensure accurate data entry.

The Society of Thoracic Surgeons (STS) maintains a robust national database that provides data on the results of specific surgeries performed by cardiothoracic surgeons. Patients can use the database to find the highest-ranked surgeon or institution for their particular procedure. Surgeons in the STS database are given ratings (of one to three stars) based on the results of the surgeries they have performed.

My team has helped me receive a three-star rating as a lung surgeon over the coveted three-year span. In fact, we even wrote an article on how to achieve this great honor. While I am proud of this fact and our team's achievement, the truth is that, in some ways, one can game the system. We know which aspects of our performance are being measured, and we can perform accordingly so that the data consistently shows optimal outcomes. I call this "pitching to the umpire strike's

---

3 https://www.researchgate.net/publication/299474654_Big_Data_Validation_
and_Quality_Assurance_-_Isssues_Challenges_and_Needs

zone." As society's yardstick for measuring true quality gets better, the ability to game the system decreases.

Database Communication

As mentioned above, a major roadblock to accessing the potential of big data is the fact that the various databases don't talk to one another. For instance, I'm a medical consultant for CHS, which is one of the largest, for-profit healthcare companies in the United States. Hospital systems like CHS generate unbelievable amounts of data, but it is only shared with their hospitals and physicians.

While some of this data is proprietary information and should remain private, some of it would be extremely beneficial for the entire healthcare industry if it were shared. Their data on the measures they are taking to ensure that patients receive better care, and their data tracking personalized treatment plans, could serve as a model for other facilities. If organizations like CHS had an incentive to share this type of data with Medicare systems, millions of patients might benefit.

Even if some organizations choose to share their data, there are so many different databases used that it would be difficult to establish meaningful data sharing. The table below lists a small fraction of the alphabet soups of the hundreds of medical databases currently being used:[4]

---

4 http://infolab.stanford.edu/pub/gio/1980/CS-TR-80-790.pdf

CCSS	CIS
CLINFO	COSTAR
GEMISCH	GMDB
FAME	IDMS
IMS	LIM
MDAS	MSAR
MUMPS	OCIS
PROMIS	RISS
Medicare.gov	AIDSource
NSQ	GeneBank
CancerCare	SPEER

Kaiser Permanente, Hospital Corp. of America, and Community Health Services utilize some of the largest databases in the country. None of these communicate with one another. We cannot solve our healthcare crisis until we encourage and reimburse data sharing between companies and improve transparency. These companies will probably protest that they don't want to share their data with their competitors, but they are likely to participate if they have the right incentives.

Chronic Disease and Pre-existing Conditions

We will see the positive effects of big data on both quality and cost of care when it comes to the management of chronic disease. High blood pressure, congestive heart failure, COPD, and diabetes are the four most common health problems in the US.[5] In fact, according to the Centers for Disease Control and Prevention (CDC), chronic diseases are "the leading causes of death and disability in the United States."[6] Chronic disease is a major financial drain on the healthcare industry. Approximately $2.7 trillion is spent annually on medical care for chronic disease.[7]

The majority of chronic diseases may be preventable and are greatly impacted by patient lifestyle. The first step we can take reduce these costs is to set up a system that encourages greater patient engagement on the financial side of health care. We must first prove that the patient has made poor lifestyle decisions and that the disease has developed due to these decisions.

In my opinion, this process is not very complicated for emphysema or for liver failure from alcoholism. Databases can monitor patients who smoke, remain overweight, take intravenous drugs, and/or neglect regular visits with their doctors or who don't follow their diet guidelines.

People are free to make these decisions, of course, but they should have a greater financial investment in the treatment of the diseases that develop from their decisions. Most decisions

---

5 https://www.cdc.gov/chronicdisease/overview/index.htm

6 https://www.cdc.gov/chronicdisease/overview/index.htm

7 http://www.bankrate.com/finance/insurance/cost-of-chronic-disease-1.aspx

we make in life carry consequences. Why would decisions related to our health not affect what we pay for our health care? When we sign up for employer healthcare coverage, we are rarely asked if we smoke, have more than a few drinks of alcohol a day, exercise routinely, or use intravenous drugs.

Many factors that are beyond our control do contribute to our susceptibility to certain health conditions, such as economic status, race, and ethnicity. But it is imperative to the future of our healthcare system that patients have monetary risk associated with healthcare needs directly resulting from their decisions. Structuring healthcare costs so that people who have made poor lifestyle decisions pay for a greater percentage of their health care could eliminate the ongoing debates about pre-existing conditions and healthcare policy.

These rules should not apply to children who are less than sixteen years of age. Too many young patients are victims of poor socio-economic upbringing and are not completely responsible for some of these choices. However, personal responsibility does become a fact of life at some point as we grow older.

Big data will play a valuable role in determining whether a pre-existing condition is caused by the patient's behaviors and lifestyle decisions. This information can then be used to determine whether the patient should be responsible for a greater portion of his or her healthcare costs. If a patient has diabetes because he chose to eat poorly and not exercise, then he should carry greater financial responsibility for his health care. If the patient was born with diabetes, of course, he would not be asked to pay more.

Smart watches, smart mattresses, smart scales, and other personal tracking devices also generate a great deal of data that can contribute to effective preventive care and the management of disease. These will play a large role in the future of healthcare reform. The concerns here are the extent of personal information being collected, how the information is shared, and with whom.

In the future, some health information will be shared directly with physicians through online applications similar to WAZE, which collects traffic information from drivers. Medical tracking apps will collect data on when patients wake up, when they go to bed, when they drink alcohol or coffee and how much, and their baseline heart rate and weight. This information will be shared with insurance companies that help determine patient healthcare fees based on behaviors.

Soon, all of our data will be embedded in chips within our bodies that will revolutionize the maintenance of EMRs (electronic medical records). Technology already exists that allows implanted chips to provide data to MDs in the emergency room if a patient is comatose. EMR chips allow us to write new data to a patient's record with a wand-like device that never pierces the skin.

While this big data will be beneficial to the healthcare industry, we will face the challenge of finding ways to maintain the privacy of personal medical information. In my opinion, we have allowed compliance officers and rules and regulation to delay progress in this area—but eventually, this is our future. Big data collected in new and novel ways is the future of health care.

Report Cards for Doctors

Big data will shape the future of the healthcare industry in other ways as well, including increased accountability for doctors. Doctors will receive report cards and will be rewarded accordingly. For example, it is known that tight regulation of blood glucose for patients with diabetes helps prevent some complications of this chronic disease. A blood test called the A1C represents how high the patient's blood glucose was over a period of time. In general, the lower the A1C, the better the patient is controlling diabetes.

Doctors who are able to keep their patients' hemoglobin A1C under seven will receive a form of incentive pay. We can use big data to look at height, weight, BMI, and so forth, as well as diet. If a patient is more engaged than most, then the physician should get credit for engaging that person. If physicians are incentivized to provide this level of care, we will see an increase in engagement among patients. That means we doctors will be, in part, responsible for how our patients behave.

Many might argue that certain doctors will receive higher rankings or achieve better results because they happen to have financially well-off patients who are in better shape than most and are more engaged in their health care. However, big data will allow us to identify socio-economic information as well. We will be able to factor in these conditions as well as the outcomes. Then we can incentivize doctors to continue providing high quality and expert care.

Doctor report cards will yield powerful results, but implementing them will be challenging. One issue is that it will be much easier to give report cards to surgeons than to medical doctors because surgeons work with more quantifiable start and end times. When I'm performing an operation, it is absolutely clear when the operation begins and ends. This simplifies the process of determining the relationship between the operation's length and specific outcomes, such as whether the patient survived, whether they experienced excessive bleeding, and whether they needed to stay in the ICU afterward. This data can be objectively observed and easily recorded, and it is difficult to manipulate.

But the true value of an operation is its durability and quality of life it offers. In a cancer surgery, the five-year survival rate based on the pathologic stage also is a factor in value. Most surgeries are evaluated with thirty-day or ninety-day metrics, but the only way to truly assess the value of any healthcare intervention is to take a longer view.

Short-term evaluations shortchange the concept of value. The money saved by preventing recurrent cancer and other expensive readmissions figures into value, but so do medical complications and the patient's pain level. These things have to be assessed over at least a five-year period.

A medical doctor treating diabetes does not have a clear start or end date—it is not always clear when the patient's diabetes began to develop or how long it went undiagnosed and untreated. For diabetes, treatment results and other outcomes are not as easily identifiable, but we can measure the number of times the patient has been hospitalized and the complications (such as the development of circulation, vision, or kidney problems) caused by the disease.

The cause-and-effect of care might be more challenging to ascertain. Implementing report cards for physicians would require planning and collaboration among experts in the field. In order to get MDs on board, report cards would have to be fair and verifiable.

Stakeholder Alignment

Big data will enable us to provide quality care and lower costs by supporting stakeholder alignment. Hospitals will benefit by recruiting highly scored physicians and surgeons, who will be more easily identifiable once we implement accurate doctor report cards that measure outcomes based on treatment quality. Hospitals can then give their medical staff incentives to maintain high scores and use data to track their results. Such information is often kept on online "dashboards," which are being used by many top-scoring hospitals such as New York University Langone Medical Center.

Doctors will benefit from big data in terms of becoming more aligned with other stakeholders. Some doctors may resist initially, as these changes will require greater accountability. They might be skeptical that their grades are truly in their own hands, and that they won't be accountable for things beyond their control, such as the patient's other risk factors and socio-economic status.

The data will allow us to more easily identify which actions, results, and behaviors lead to higher rankings and more pay. Further, incorporating big data into the medical industry will actually empower healthcare providers to take a more active role in what is being measured and how.

Big data will also assist in aligning all of the stakeholders by increasing transparency when comes to healthcare costs. A patient should be able to look up the cost of a lobectomy in New York City by Robert Cerfolio and see exactly how many he has done, what his outcomes have been, how many lymph nodes he takes out, how many of his patients are re-admitted, and what their pain is like two, five, or seven days after the surgery.

Once we align financial data with clinical and administrative data, we will draw valuable conclusions that will increase alignment among all stakeholders. As this level of data improves and is tweaked again and again to make it more reflective of superior care, it will drive physician behavior to better performance. This, in turn, will generate greater profits for hospitals. Hospital administrators will be aligned to ensure that their data is accurately presented and that new metrics of quality are frequently added to better account for patient risk factors. All the while, the patients will benefit by receiving continually improving care.

In Conclusion

Data that is accurate and that measures meaningful metrics ultimately will drive behavior. This is how big data is going to help us devise solutions for the problems we're experiencing today.

I've already described one way I saw big data used to help improve value. During my time at the University of Alabama, I was honored to serve as the Chair of the Business Intelligence Team. We were able to significantly improve outcomes by collecting accurate data and presenting it to our physicians and surgeons in a granular and specific manner. The data included operative notes as well as information on the time discharge orders were written in the morning—and the latter enabled us to free up beds for patients coming out of surgery.

The information we collected made it easy to identify the areas in which each doctor needed to improve, and that helped improve the entire healthcare system—and that, subsequently, improved individual patient care. When information is specific and undeniable, it often motivates professionals to improve their procedures.

Accurate big data at this level will also minimize complaints about the ranking systems, because we will not be able to make excuses for our scores. We will be held accountable to numbers that we supply. We will be evaluated based on metrics that we have all agreed are clinically meaningful and reflective of the level of our care.

Chapter 5

REGIONAL MEDICAL COURTS–
NOT JUST TORT REFORM

Tort reform and its overall impact on
our healthcare system have recently received some attention—
but not enough. In states that have implemented tort reform,
we have begun to see its beneficial effect on healthcare costs.

American Action Forum (AAF), a Washington, D.C.-based
conservative think tank, found that multiple-state medical
liability reforms reduced employer healthcare costs by 3.5
percent.[1] But while tort reform is a step in the right direction,
it is not the final answer.

I am probably one of the few cardiothoracic surgeon to have
performed more than 17,500 operations and never been sued.
However, I do medical expert legal reviews. I have never seen a

---

1 https://www.americanactionforum.org/research/tort-reforms-impact-health-
care-costs/

more inefficient, expensive, drawn-out, non-lean process in my life than the current system for filing lawsuits against physicians.

Simple cases that are completely frivolous—and known to be so by everyone—drag on for years and years. Dates for depositions are changed and delayed and canceled all the time, as are court dates.

Even more incredibly, when a legal case does finally go to court, they'll find that court is in session for just a few hours. I've been there for only three such cases. The docket doesn't even begin until eight or nine in the morning—two to three hours later than most operating rooms start—and they break for an entire hour for lunch. Then they adjourn at four pm. No industry could survive this type of culture except for one subsided by the federal government.

The court experience for physicians is incredible stressful, even in cases where most people agree that they did nothing wrong. Medical malpractice lawsuits and the fear of being sued currently dictate many of our healthcare procedures and processes. The AMA estimates that, for every hundred physicians now in practice, an average of ninety-five medical malpractice lawsuits have been filed.[2] The looming fear fostered by these statistics has given rise to "defensive" medicine.

Defensive medicine means that MDs order tests that might not really benefit the patients or improve their care,

2 http://abcnews.go.com/Health/HealthCare/malpractice-lawsuits-doctors-common-ama/story?id=11332146

but are ordered so that someday we can argue in court that we ordered all the needed tests (plus some). These irrelevant or unnecessary tests and procedures drive up costs without providing any clinical value.

For example, if a patient has a lung cancer and is asymptomatic for a metastatic lesion in the brain (no headaches or other central nervous system symptoms), some physicians will still order a brain scan. Our experience and training tell us that there is only a 1 to 2 percent chance that the patient has a lesion on the brain if a CT and PET scan show an early-stage, non-small-cell lung cancer. To order a brain CT or MRI in this situation is a poor expenditure of time and money that could be spent better helping other patients. But some doctors will order the brain scan to protect against future lawsuits by the 1 to 2 percent.

Defensive medicine requires that these tests be done so that they can be used as evidence in a potential future malpractice suit. This is such a common phenomenon that an estimated 26 to 34 percent of annual healthcare costs can be attributed to defensive medicine.[3] As annual healthcare spending in the US has hit $3.8 trillion,[4] we're looking at more than $1 trillion a year spent just on defensive medicine.

We need to enact reforms that reduce the power malpractice lawsuits currently hold over the healthcare industry. It's

---

3 http://www.healthcarefinancenews.com/news/defensive-medicine-adds-650b-850b-annual-healthcare-costs

4 https://www.forbes.com/sites/danmunro/2014/02/02/annual-u-s-healthcare-spending-hits-3-8-trillion/#124382f576a9

important to note that both lawyers *and* physicians (myself included—as I'll explain in the next section) have benefitted economically from the current system for dealing with medical malpractice. The situation that we are in can't be blamed on any one person or group, but all of us who are involved in the healthcare industry can play a role in improving it.

We need an entire culture change as a critical part of solving this aspect of the high cost of US health care. In this chapter, we'll explore possible solutions.

Medical Malpractice in Court

I serve as an expert witness in five to ten medical malpractice cases every year, and this experience has given me a great deal of insight into the business of malpractice suits.

Participating in malpractice cases as an expert witness pays a lot of money for very little work. For example, I took a phone call last night in which I merely stated my opinion on a pending malpractice case; for those twenty minutes of my time, I was paid $3,500. For depositions, I am paid about $1,200 an hour. These are exorbitant amounts of money compared to the amount of work required, and these fees serve to illustrate the amount of profit tied to malpractice suits. The 2016 Medical Malpractice Annual Report found that insurers and self-insurers spent $67.9 million defending lawsuits.[5]

---

5 https://www.insurance.wa.gov/about-oic/reports/commissioner-reports/documents/2016-med-mal- annual-report.pdf

Furthermore, the medical malpractice court system is extremely inefficient. Because of short workdays and long breaks for judges and jurors, the courts have accumulated a massive backlog of malpractice cases. Each case takes anywhere from six months to more than a year.[6]

One change that we could implement immediately would be to shift the current nine a.m. to four p.m. court schedule to seven a.m. to seven p.m., so that we can get these cases up to date. This is the same time frame most operating rooms use. And yes, we have work to do after hours, just like lawyers have work to do when the courtroom day ends.

In my capacity as an expert, I go to court, give depositions, read case-related materials, and review files. What I have found through these experiences is that most of the cases I'm involved in aren't actually due to malpractice. True malpractice cases are rare. The only people who benefit from filing most of these suits are the lawyers and expert witnesses. On average, patients who win medical malpractice claims receive more than $1.1 million,[7] and their lawyers get up to 40 percent of that payout.[8]

The loss of wages and the medical costs involved in malpractice cases generally do not warrant such large payouts. While

---

6 http://www.lawfirms.com/resources/medical-malpractice/medical-negligence-lawsuits/length-process.htm

7 https://www.insurance.wa.gov/about-oic/reports/commissioner-reports/documents/2016-med-mal-annual-report.pdf

8 http://law.freeadvice.com/malpractice_law/medical_malpractice/medical-malpractice-contingency-fee.htm

many lawyers only take on meaningful cases, others push disgruntled patients to file malpractice suits regardless of the validity of their cases. To be honest, almost all the attorneys I meet are hard-working, honest people. They agree that the entire climate and culture surrounding malpractice lawsuits needs revamping.

Perhaps due to unrealistic expectations, many patients are prepared to sue whenever there is an undesirable outcome—regardless of the cause. In medicine, our outcomes often are not ideal, even when patients have received very good care.

We need to adjust our system so that it protects victims of malpractice while also protecting our system from abuse. Caps on the amount that can be awarded are one solution, but there are others.

The Solutions

As stated before, I have personally performed more than 17,700 operations, and I have never been sued. However, this record is nearly unheard-of for a cardio-thoracic surgeon. More than 60 percent of doctors over the age of fifty-five in the US have been sued at least once for malpractice, and surgeons are five times more likely to be sued than most medical doctors.[9]

One possible solution is to move healthcare-related disputes to tribunals that allow non-conflicted doctors to decide the

9 https://www.medpagetoday.com/practicemanagement/
practicemanagement/21534

outcomes of cases. If done correctly, these tribunals would help reduce defensive medicine and cap liability claims in lawsuits, allowing for several improvements across the board.

The costs would go down dramatically, since no tribunal would pay a physician $1,200 an hour to testify. Medical tribunals would reduce the number of malpractice lawsuits, which in turn would reduce expenditures on insurance and legal issues. Reducing such costs would allow hospitals and physicians to invest more in tools and skills that would improve the quality of care that patients receive.

Medical tribunals would necessitate the implementation of safeguards to ensure that doctors who are being sued do not have an unfair advantage. I believe we are capable of creating an atmosphere in which malpractice suits are reviewed fairly and efficiently.

Independent boards made up of doctors who are also lawyers (of which there are an increasing number)—as well as physicians who are no longer practicing—would ensure expert evaluation of each case. Another way to ensure objectivity in these tribunals would be to pay the physicians who serve on the board a set salary that is in no way tied to the outcome of any case.

The tribunals would be made up of physicians who are experts in their fields, along with nurses, administrators, and lawyers. These experts would be vetted so that there is no conflict of interest with the patient or physician involved in the case.

These boards would meet monthly or biweekly, as necessary, so that cases could be reviewed and decided upon quickly.

Cases found to be frivolous or fraudulent would be thrown out immediately.

One question regarding these tribunals is whether patients would have the right to sue in legal court after a board of experts deemed a malpractice case to be unsubstantiated. In order for this solution to have teeth, the decision of the tribunal should be binding. However, we cannot restrict patients from going to court or working with other lawyers. Our hope is that the tribunals would possess sufficient power to make a difference in the number of malpractice lawsuits we are currently experiencing.

We would need to work out several details in order to implement medical tribunals. The important first step is to discuss the possibilities for changing our current system. The cost of an inefficiently run system does not end with financial losses; the system also takes a toll on the emotional well-being of all involved. The tribunals will alleviate this hardship and streamline the process. Further, when malpractice suits are won, patients will directly receive all damage awards instead of handing over large percentages to their lawyers.

Others have proposed medical tribunals in the past, but they have been rejected by policymakers who don't want to eliminate an income source for thousands of attorneys. In light of this, the best solution might be a compromise: Medical malpractice cases could go through the tribunals, and only those cases deemed to have sufficient merit would continue to court with representation by malpractice lawyers.

We can phase out the malpractice courts over time, but this does not need to be an immediate or sudden change. The attorneys who specialize in medical malpractice cases will have the time and opportunities necessary to evolve their careers along with these changes, just as any industry must when disruptive change enters the market.

Back to Alignment

The legal system we have in place for medical malpractice lawsuits today demonstrates another example of the need for alignment among the stakeholders. For example, as costly as defensive medicine is, hospitals still push for unnecessary tests and procedures because they know these test results might help avert lawsuits—and because tests are moneymakers for the hospital systems. Every patient who gets an MRI generates significant income for the hospitals system. If you had paid millions of capital dollars for an MRI machine, would you want it to sit idle, or would you find ways to use it?

Insurance companies end up paying more for unnecessary tests as well, and physicians are required to administer and document these tests, even if the test wasn't completely necessary. The patient also loses in this situation, because he or she ends up spending time and energy on unnecessary procedures.

The reality is that most everyone is afraid of being sued. The patient often does not have enough information on the costs, impact, or reasons for most tests and procedures. The physicians have a lot of documents to sign, most of which are required by the hospital legal and compliance team to help protect the MD. Many physicians see the compliance officer, whose job it is to protect both doctor and hospital, as an enemy.

This culture leads to system paralysis because of the unnecessary procedures and paperwork. Just think of all the people you meet and all the forms you must sign before you have a simple operation. Imagine how surgeons feel having to go through all that red tape and unnecessary triple and quadruple checks, day after day, just to get you into the operating room. It is a total waste of valuable time for patients, doctors, and hospitals.

Reducing the legal profession's impact on the healthcare industry, as well as the voluminous compliance forms, will help to better align all the stakeholders. If we can agree that the highest quality of care for the patient at the lowest cost possible is our goal, then we have to stop ordering tests that do not provide quality or value. We have to stop wasting the healthcare provider's time documenting things that add little value to the patient's care. Research reported recently in Forbes Magazine showed that physicians spend 49.2 percent of their time on paperwork and documentation.[10]

With a common goal, anything that is safe and beneficial for one of the stakeholders will also be safe and beneficial for the others. We need to be able to prove the necessity of

---

10 https://www.forbes.com/sites/brucelee/2016/09/07/doctors-wasting-over-two-thirds-of-their-time-doing-paperwork/#771212505d7b

tests, procedures, and policies in order to fulfill our goal and maintain alignment.

We cannot allow the legal system to do this, because legislation and litigation are costly for all of us, and they push us further from our goal. Once we align stakeholders, we'll be able to decrease the cost of health care without reducing its quality.

In Conclusion

The implementation of tort reform and medical tribunals will reduce the power of the legal system in health care and allow for new opportunities in the delivery of care. One feature of recent conversations about health care is *bundled care*—a system under which an insurance company would provide the hospital, the physician, or the patient with a lump sum for his or her specific illness or disease and let them decide how best to allocate those funds.

In bundled care, the physician would want to order the most necessary tests and the most efficient procedures to treat the patient, without having to practice "defensive medicine." The hospital would approve those procedures. The patient would benefit from high-quality care, and the insurance company would not have to pay for unnecessary tests. Once they are liberated from the fear of potential lawsuits, hospitals and physicians will embrace bundled care as an opportunity to provide quality care at lower costs.

Medical tribunals will give rise to changes throughout the healthcare industry that will bring patients, physicians, hospitals, and lawyers into alignment. The glut of malpractice suits will subside, and with it, the practice of defensive medicine. Attorneys can serve as advisors in the review of medical cases, and patients will receive high-quality care. As a result, insurance companies will pay less, and physicians will determine what tests and procedures are necessary. Hospitals will streamline processes with protocols, and MDs will be able to spend more time with patients and less time typing into computers or dictating into microphones.

Any change that brings us closer to alignment in this way will bring us closer to solving the healthcare crisis. The most important step we can take to achieve this future is to have solutions-oriented, collaborative conversations.

Chapter 6

THE POWER OF METRICS

METRICS ARE EXTREMELY POWERFUL, AND AS with big data, we should examine how they are shaping the future of our healthcare system. To fully realize the power of metrics, we need to consider two points.

First, metrics can determine how people behave. And second, metrics are a pre-requisite to change. Or, as my three boys have heard me say a thousand times:

"What an organization measures and what they reward determine their culture."

and

"You have to finds ways to accurately measure something before you can improve it."

The questions that then arise are, *What should we be measuring?* and *What use should we make of the results we obtain from measurement?* In this chapter, we'll look into these questions and explore the power of metrics in guiding healthcare policy.

As mentioned previously, the future of health care is going to focus on quality, not volume. Once quality is valued over quantity on an industry-wide scale, physicians and surgeons will not be paid based on the number of procedures they perform or patients they see; their paychecks will be based on the *outcomes* of these procedures, visits, and treatments.

Physicians and surgeons are highly competitive individuals; they have to be in order to successfully get into and graduate from medical school, and to secure top-tier residencies, fellowships, and internships. So when a system supplies incentives for *results*, doctors will quickly improve their scores in those measured outcomes.

Culture is determined by what is measured and how funds are allocated. For instance, my culture and values would be apparent to anyone who visits my home. I have a batting cage, a football field, a basketball court, a large swimming pool, and a three-hole, par 3, sixty- to seventy-yard golf course. It's immediately obvious that I value not only character and academics, but also sports. I measure myself by my ability to perform well at sports. I also value my kids' work ethic and school grades, so I invest in those aspects of their lives.

These metrics determine the culture of my home. They are why my boys have been so incredibly successful in school and athletics. These principles are true when applied to the healthcare industry as well.

Current Obstacles

This notion of measuring quality over volume is not new, but conversations about this topic often raise concerns. The problem is that stakeholders cannot agree on which metrics should be used to measure the level of care that hospitals and physicians deliver. If we grade hospitals based on patients' length of stay, surgeons and medical physicians will have an incentive to get patients discharged as quickly as possible—which is not always in a patient's best interest.

Patient satisfaction is another metric that may be used to measure quality; but how can we measure patient satisfaction? I've been affiliated with hospitals that handed out surveys to measure how satisfied patients were with their quality of care—and found that the determining factor was often the hospital food. The second factor was available parking, perhaps because family members usually help the patient complete the survey, and if there isn't any parking available or they had to pay for parking, it becomes a point of dissatisfaction.

In reality, if you are a great surgeon but work at a hospital with bad food and limited parking, your scores might be low. Because surveys do not accurately reflect the quality of care, they are an unreliable metric.

When irrelevant metrics reflect poorly on physicians and hospitals, it can lead to a backlash, generating processes and procedures that are not always conducive to quality care. Another factor patients use to determine quality of care is how nurses and physicians respond to their pain. If a patient presses the call button to report pain and a nurse doesn't immediately show up with pain-relieving medication—or if the nurse says the patient cannot be given any more medication at that time—this leads to poor reviews. In order to avoid low ratings from patients, hospitals may instruct the doctors to prescribe narcotics for pain management. This might have been a factor in the epidemic of patients who are now addicted to prescription narcotics. It is estimated that more than 15 million people in the US abuse prescription drugs.[1]

Hospitals need high scores to maintain their ratings, to bring in top-tier physicians, and to secure funding. They also need good reviews to encourage patients to choose them for their care. Yet many platforms that are used to measure patient satisfaction in the public domain—such as Self Graders, Yelp, and Health Grades—are really only measures of whether the patient *likes* the physician. Patients usually like a doctor best when the doctor gives them what they want. Physicians know that if they say to a patient, "Listen, I know you're in a little bit of pain, but you'd be better off using over-the-counter pain medication," they will likely receive poor ratings.

I frequently have this conversation with my own patients, because they don't understand why I won't renew their narcotic prescriptions. I always offer another form of pain-reducing medication that is not addictive, but patients in pain won't

1 https://talbottcampus.com/2015-prescription-drug-abuse-statistics/

believe that a milder drug will be effective enough. This dilemma occurs with antibiotics as well. Every patient who has a cough calls the office for antibiotics—but I haven't prescribed one in twenty-one years. This is partly because I'm a surgeon, but also because I refuse to prescribe an antibiotic just so the patient leaves happy. I'd rather spend ten minutes explaining why an antibiotic won't help their viral infection and persuading them that an antibiotic can have negative side effects. A lot of doctors do this, but it's time-consuming—and it can lead to low scores.

In addition to examining which metrics are measured, we must also adjust how data is collected, validated, and reported. Metrics should be reported to independent medical societies, not to the healthcare industry or a government agency. Independent medical societies are the most unbiased option to set the appropriate metrics and quality indices, review the data, ensure its accuracy, and award grades. An independent society can then present this data to the public so patients can make informed decisions about their health care. This is what the Society of Thoracic Surgeons database tries to do for heart and lung surgeons, and it works well.

Valuable Metrics

These examples demonstrate that we must adjust our metrics so they truly measure the quality of care patients are receiving. We have mentioned readmission as an appropriate way to measure quality of care, instead of measuring length of stay. Most patients do not want to be readmitted; the doctor doesn't want the patient readmitted and the hospital doesn't want the patient readmitted; and the insurance company doesn't want to pay for patients who are readmitted, either. This is a metric of quality that all of the stakeholders can agree upon, which means all stakeholders are in alignment. However, social issues at home sometimes mean the patient's family cannot deliver the care the patient needs, and without alternatives for care, readmissions become necessary. To keep readmissions low, we would need to develop more available alternatives, such as short-term nursing home or assisted living care.

What kind of metrics could be used to evaluate different types of physicians? For surgery, one metric might be how long it takes the surgeon to perform a specific operation. The second metric would be the amount of blood loss the patient experiences. A third metric might be specific to cancer-related operations—how many lymph nodes were removed at the time of the operation. The lymph nodes are important to stage some types of patients with cancer. The fourth metric, also specific to a cancer operation, might be whether all of the cancer was taken out. We call this an "R0 resection." Surgeons who do not consistently rank well by these metrics probably are not providing a high quality of care.

Another metric we can use to measure quality of care for doctors who treat cancer patients is whether chemotherapy was prescribed for a patient within two weeks of their death. The thinking is that, if a patient is prescribed chemotherapy but only survives an additional two weeks, then perhaps the physician should have recognized their dire situation and placed them in hospice care sooner.

We recently began using a metric of whether the patient's cancer was completely clinically staged within ten business days after the first appointment. The problem with this one is, speed of staging often reflects how well the hospital system can do tests like scans and lab work—not the MD's quality of care.

A metric of success for doctors who specialize in treating patients with diabetes—an example we will use thought out this book—is the patients' A1C[2] levels, as well as hospital admissions and readmissions. Of course, good blood sugar control also relies on the patients being compliant by controlling their diets and taking their medication. An uncooperative patient's high A1C scores would reflect poorly on the physician. However, the best physicians find ways to encourage their patients to take their diabetes seriously, and if you have enough patients, the non-compliant ones will wash out in the final analysis.

Not only are these metrics detailed and closely related to quality, but they are also objective. Neither physicians nor hospitals can "game the system" with most of these metrics. Over time, we will define new metrics and tweak the old ones to make them more reflective of true quality care.

---

2 The A1C test is a blood test that provides information about a patient's average levels of blood glucose over the past three months. (National Institutes of Health) https://www.niddk.nih.gov/health-information/diabetes/overview/tests-diagnosis/a1c-test

Our vision is for each specialty to define and report its own metrics, as well as improve the risk stratification that goes into each one. The best metrics are definable and comparable across institutions and countries. To find solutions, we need to be specific and think in terms of measurable outcomes.

The Solutions

One way to fairly and accurately measure the quality of care is to have experts in each specialty determine which objectives and outcomes will be measured per procedure, treatment, or disease. This information would be collected into a validated database, and we could then begin scoring what matters.

We envision each specialty also forming bodies that help collect the data as well as house it and ensure it has been entered accurately. This is already done in my specialty, cardio-thoracic surgery, by the Society of Thoracic Surgery (STS) database—but the process is not always in alignment with other specialties. For example, one very important metric for cancer surgery is the five-year survival rate—but the quality of care for surgery is currently measured by the STS at thirty to ninety days after the operation. We should be looking at how the patient has done a month after surgery but also five years after surgery.

One potential difficulty with these kinds of metrics is the problem of fairness. Doctors are less likely to have successful outcomes if their practices serve patients who have lower socioeconomic backgrounds, poor nutrition, and less access to other medical care. This puts them at an unfair disadvantage.

But social advantages exist in every system. It isn't necessarily fair that my three kids had parents who could pay $3,000 for them to take ACT-review courses that helped them earn high scores, which got them accepted into Ivy League schools. Many families cannot afford these courses or private tutors—and that is absolutely not fair. Whenever there is a system of any kind in place, people with a higher socioeconomic status have an inevitable advantage. We get to game the system.

This is true within the healthcare industry as well. If we are basing specific metrics on surgery outcomes, doctors in higher-income neighborhoods and in urban areas will have an advantage. The reality is that a doctor in a small town in Nebraska cannot choose his or her patients as carefully as I can. That doctor will be operating on a larger percentage of older and sicker patients, which will significantly affect the outcomes of her surgeries.

Like many academic general thoracic surgeons, I have seen many of the oldest and sickest patients with the largest cancers—but I can offer them other options besides surgery, while physicians in smaller communities might not be able to do that. With my high volume of patients, I can choose whom to operate on and decide who might benefit from radiation instead. It isn't fair, but it is the reality of the system we are working in.

As surgical leaders, we will have the opportunity to determine which variables are of value and how they will be measured. Physicians must determine what factors will go into trying to make the system as equitable as we can. It is our responsibility to choose these metrics carefully and with expert attention, so they measure what they are supposed to: health care at high quality and low cost.

Metrics Guiding Health Care

Once we've carefully gathered and measured these metrics, we will use this information to guide healthcare policy through specific process improvements. Metrics will help us use root-cause analysis to improve our many processes.

Here's an example: Several years ago, we found that too many people were contracting pneumonia after surgery. We monitored the situation and began making adjustments to our processes until post-op pneumonia was almost a non-issue. The changes we made included making the incisions a little bit smaller, hiring a respiratory therapist, and adding additional nurses to ensure that patients were walking more. These changes took our scores back up to three stars on the STS database scoring system. This is the power of metrics.

We can use metrics to identify the best caregivers as well as those who are mediocre. The best will be given more patients and will be asked to share their processes and procedures with the healthcare industry, to improve the quality of care across the board. Those who are found to be mediocre will learn and develop through industry conferences and through workplace visits to and from experts.

In this way, professionals in the field who are earning three stars will be teaching those who are earning two stars, giving the lower-rated individuals the opportunity to grow, which is beneficial to every stakeholder.

We have a three-star-rated program at my hospital now, but the reality is that we are—at all times—just one death or one pneumonia case away from becoming a two-star program. Our rating was based on 212 hospitals that reported data over a three-year period. In order to be graded, a center had to do at least twenty lobectomies (lung removal surgeries) for lung cancer. Only 12 of the 212 hospitals received a three-star ranking. With numbers this small, the difference between a three-star rating and a two-star rating is one bacterium or a single avoidable, adverse outcome.

In medicine, there is always an element of luck—but if poor outcomes continue to happen, year after year, it probably has less to do with luck and more to do with processes or procedures that need to be improved. The beauty of quality data is that it tells you where you are and what deficits you have, so you know where you need to improve.

Competition among professionals and hospitals is healthy because it forces us to push ourselves to deliver higher quality care. But it's important to keep in mind that the bottom line is always patient care. If teaching other hospitals or doctors our improvements, processes, or novel methods means that more patients are going to have access to great care, then that's what we need to be doing. We are competing for customers, but we ultimately we want everyone to receive high-quality care.

In Conclusion

As we continue to make improvements to our metrics, we will be able to direct patients to centers of excellence. If a hospital's neurosurgical program continues to be rated with one star, over time, the lack of customers going there should lead to its closure—but only if potential patients know the hospital is a consistent under-performer.

When we drive large numbers of patients to a place that is performing well, they begin performing even better. They are able to specialize in one area, practice it constantly, and develop novel techniques that truly work. This drives down costs as well, because we can buy more material at a cheaper price.

Probably most importantly, we reduce cost with high volume because we become protocol-driven. I have a protocol for everything after lung and esophageal cancer surgery, because we have seen it all a hundred times in the past and we know the best way to prevent problems and/or to deal with them if they happen.

The power of metrics will provide us with information that we can use to continually improve centers of excellence and close poorly operating centers. In the end, all the stakeholders will benefit, because the healthcare industry overall will experience lower costs and deliver a higher quality of care.

In using metrics, we would be shifting this aspect of health care toward a more European model. I recently went to Germany as a visiting professor at a center that specialized in thymectomies.[3] The physicians there performed several of these surgeries a day. Nearly everyone in Germany who needs a thymectomy is sent to this center, and the lead physician there is exceptionally skilled in this procedure. This is an example of how some of the European healthcare systems develop centers of excellence.

Once you have fairly identified centers of excellence and closed centers that aren't up to par, patients, insurance companies, physicians, and hospitals all benefit. Some hospitals will end up closing their doors, but the ones that are truly providing a public service will thrive. Instead of trying to provide every service at every facility, hospitals will have centers that specialize in particular procedures and services. Those centers will be so profitable that they won't mind referring patients to other hospitals if they need something different.

As metrics affect how people behave, we can use them to guide stakeholder behavior that supports improvements within our healthcare system. As long as we are able to measure something, we are able to improve it. So let's measure our system, starting with our hospitals and physicians.

---

3 Surgical removal of the thymus gland.

Chapter 7

EFFECTIVELY MANAGING CHRONIC DISEASE

CHRONIC DISEASE IS THE LEADING CAUSE OF death and disability in the US,[1] so the way we manage it is of utmost importance. Yet the lack of alignment among stakeholders within the healthcare industry is exacerbating the already poor management of chronic disease.

We will need to take several steps to create a healthcare system that effectively manages chronic disease: First, we must accurately assess the quality of care that patients with chronic disease are receiving.

Quality can be assessed and graded by using the equation:

value = quality/ cost

and therefore:

quality = (value) x (cost)

---

1 https://www.cdc.gov/chronicdisease/overview/index.htm

Physicians can decide fair metrics to assess the quality of care for a specific disease and use metrics to determine individual patient risk scores. In this way, they can fairly assess the quality of their treatment interventions and score their own performances.

We also must create metrics that drive stakeholder behavior toward the proper management of chronic disease—and we must hold both physicians and patients accountable for their part in the management of chronic disease.

In Chapters 4 and 6, we explored the potential of big data and metrics to resolve many of the issues healthcare systems face today. We also looked into several ways in which we might change our metrics to ensure that physicians and hospitals have an incentive to provide quality care. While these strategies also apply to the management of chronic disease, it is more difficult to collect data and create new metrics for chronic disease because of the many variables involved. Chronic disease can vary in timeliness of diagnosis, invasiveness of the disease, and treatments available and undertaken. Most difficult to measure are patient factors: the fact that different patients have different personal variables that can affect disease outcomes. Having said this, we must find a way to measure outcomes for chronic disease. Only physicians who treat a chronic disease can accurately do this.

If we are to measure quality solely by outcomes, we cannot apply the same metrics to surgeons and physicians. As we have previously mentioned, it is easier to collect data for surgeons because an operation offers more quantifiable data, including the start and end points of surgery, amount of blood loss, amount of cancerous tissue removed, and lymph nodes removed. We can also measure readmission rate after surgery and stage-specific survival rates.

While surgeries do have some variables, they are easier to identify and account for. The patient's age and general condition would be a variable. Surgeons who operate mostly on young people with healthy hearts and lungs can expect a larger number of positive outcomes, whereas surgeons who operate on mostly elderly patients cannot expect them to do as well. All outcomes must take into account the patient's risk score. We have many models now that help us assess this risk with relative accuracy. We would ask each specialty group to devise their own risk scores and quality metrics, and continually tweak the system to further improve data accuracy.

When it comes to collecting and analyzing similar data pertaining to physicians who treat chronic disease, the process is more complex. The outcome of a physician's treatment of chronic disease greatly relies on factors beyond the doctor's control, such as the patient's genetics and behavior. Some variables in chronic disease treatment are even more difficult to identify and quantify: the patient's mental toughness, level of engagement in healing, and compliance with medication. Even the patient's culture and social support system can make a significant difference in how well their disease treatment will work. Such factors are complex, but they can be measured.

Engaged physicians can help us determine fair metrics that account for these factors.

It is also more difficult to assess the time factor in chronic diseases, because we do not always know the onset dates. Often, chronic disease has been developing for several years before diagnosis. In some cases, we might not even have an accurate date of diagnosis or information about previous treatment plans—and we might know even less about lifestyle choices or behaviors that might affect the outcome of the physician's efforts.

Despite the fact that it is more difficult to assess outcomes in patients with chronic disease, it is even more important to do so for them than it is for other types of conditions.

Measuring Outcomes

We must find appropriate metrics that we can use to measure the quality of care provided for chronic disease, which includes data on the outcome. The metrics we choose should also provide incentives for physicians and hospitals to improve treatment outcomes. In other words, we have to pick metrics that align with the hospital's financial bottom line. Only when we agree on how best to measure quality of care for chronic disease can we begin to improve patient care.

I have used patients with diabetes as an example. A physician responsible for managing diabetes should regularly test the patient's A1C blood levels, since the A1C directly correlates with how well diabetes is being controlled. Physicians can test this level—but how responsible are they for the result? Doctors often blame an elevated A1C on patient noncompliance with treatment: not taking required medication, eating a poor diet, and failing to exercise. While all of those things do affect the A1C, it is partly the physician's responsibility to engage each patient in his or her own treatment.

While there will always be some patients who refuse to get well, when the number of patients is high enough, these patients won't greatly skew the statistics. The best MDs should rise to the top of the ratings, especially if they have patients from a wide range of socioeconomic status. This is also a good example of how encouraging patients to take greater financial responsibility for their health care might increase the quality of care, because greater financial responsibility will likely promote greater patient engagement.

Another effective measure of the management of diabetes is the patient's eyesight, because uncontrolled diabetes can cause specific vision problems that can easily be identified and quantified. Documenting the patient's visual acuity, at timed intervals, is one way to accurately measure the effectiveness of the management of the disease.

If we can identify the outcomes we *don't* want, or the indicators of failing health as it pertains to a specific disease, we can use this information to measure the quality of care that physicians provide as well as the level of patient engagement. Once we decide on the appropriate metrics for measurement, we can implement best practices nationwide for the most prevalent chronic diseases. In addition to diabetes, these include heart disease, stroke, obesity, and cancer.[2]

Incentivizing Health

The complexity of chronic disease treatment presents many obstacles if we are to hold both physicians and patients accountable for its effective management. We need to account for the variables that affect the outcomes of chronic disease treatment, and we need to create novel metrics that provide incentives for both patients and physicians to effectively manage the disease.

Physicians are currently paid more money if a patient keeps coming back for more and more care. If the physician admits the patient to a hospital, he or she might make even more money. The physician has no financial incentive to keep the patient healthy and out of the hospital in our current system, although the truth is, that is what we all try to do every day.

This all goes back to a lack of stakeholder alignment: Physicians who are paid per office visit and per procedure do not have an incentive to keep patients out of the office or hospital. It is more lucrative for the physician to have the patient coming back for repeated visits.

Now, this is not to imply that physicians are intentionally hindering patient recovery or ineffectively managing chronic disease. But the reality is that physicians will find more innovative and creative ways to engage the patient and effectively

2 https://www.cdc.gov/chronicdisease/overview/

manage chronic disease if they have a financial incentive to do so. At that point, they will be better aligned with hospital and insurance companies. Similarly, patients are far more likely to engage with their own health and to take the steps necessary to effectively manage their chronic disease if they have a financial incentive, too.

Alignment

The lack of alignment among stakeholders is painfully apparent when it comes to the management of chronic disease. It may seem that hospitals would want patients with chronic disease repeatedly admitted, as this generates payment for insurance companies, but the reality is that patients with chronic disease do not generate much income for hospitals. Insurance providers like Medicare and others do not always pay for readmission and sometimes refuse to pay for certain events.

Healthcare providers have a special term—"never events"—to describe things that should never happen in a healthcare setting. Insurance companies will not pay for "never events" such as wrong-side surgery—operating on the left leg when the patient's problem was in the right leg—or for infections that occur after cardiac surgery, which can cost a hospital more than a quarter of a million dollars to treat.

Never events put hospitals at great financial risk. They have forced cardiac surgeons like my many colleagues to discover novel ways to reduce or eliminate sternal wound infections. However, the truth is, it's impossible to eliminate infections

100 percent. Such infections are almost never related to poor care, and they're an example of why many physicians are upset over these types of initiatives.

Hospitals prefer surgical patients to chronically ill patients because they make a lot more money from surgical patients. We need to find a way to give physicians an incentive to manage chronic disease so that the patient will never need to be admitted to the hospital—and to give hospitals an incentive to provide quality care to patients with chronic disease, even if they're not profitable.

Hospital and insurance companies have been studying population health programs, where providers are paid to keep patients healthy using preventive educational techniques (such as help controlling weight and quitting smoking) to prevent chronic disease. They also have the goal of more global screening tests to discover and treat diseases at early stages. Therapy is more effective when a disease is caught early, and it's much cheaper than surgical treatment or long-term care.

Some physicians *do* have an incentive to efficiently manage chronic disease. For example, physicians who are part of a bundled-care network that will only pay a specific amount of money to treat a patient with diabetes have a greater incentive to manage a diabetic patient's illness efficiently. This system works because—regardless of how many times the patient is seen, admitted, or treated—the physician receives one lump sum for treating the patient's chronic disease over the course of a year. The physician wants to engage the patient and prescribe a treatment plan that works, not just because of his compassion, but also because it is more lucrative to do so.

In this kind of system, the more compliant the patient is, and the better his overall health, the less often he comes into the office. A healthier and more compliant patient takes up less of the physician's time and resources, and does not need to be admitted to the hospital. This is why insurance companies are beginning to offer this form of bundled care. Physicians and hospitals receive a specific amount per patient per disease, and in this manner, all stakeholders are aligned to achieve results with the least amount of resources used.

Once we have the insurance companies aligned with the physician and the patient, we suggest that the patient be charged a specific amount of money for being admitted or for noncompliance with medication and treatment plans. There has to be some patient alignment in this process. Similarly, the physician will lose money every time the patient is admitted. In this way, everyone is going to want to keep the patient at home and effectively managing chronic disease. These are just examples of some of the steps that we can take in order to more effectively manage chronic disease.

This form of bundled care is slowly gaining popularity, but it is not the way that many large insurance companies—including Medicare or Medicaid—pay most physicians and hospitals. To achieve the changes needed to give all stakeholders an incentive to effectively manage chronic disease, we must create greater alignment.

Preventative Care

The CDC estimates that 86 percent of all healthcare spending is for people with one or more chronic medical conditions[3]. It would benefit the entire healthcare community to more effectively manage chronic disease. Of course, much of this starts with preventive health—no smoking, less alcohol intake, regular exercise, healthy food choices, etc.

Yet, even if every American did all of these things, starting today, we still would have many years of treating the bad decisions that patients have made over the past decades. While stakeholder alignment and the effective management of chronic disease will go a long way toward reducing healthcare costs, the most efficient way to reduce future costs is *preventative* care.

Preventative care generally means maintaining a level of health that is conducive to preventing disease or illness. For instance, we know that smoking causes emphysema; if we spent money on smoking cessation programs for teenagers and then quadrupled their cost of getting health care if they do smoke, we are providing an incentive for them not to start smoking. Despite the steady increase in the cost of cigarettes, and the fact that fewer Americans smoke every year, we still have about 20 percent of the US population addicted to nicotine. The image below shows the reduction in rates of smokers in the US:[4]

---

3 https://www.cdc.gov/chronicdisease/overview/index.htm

4 http://www.gallup.com/poll/156833/one-five-adults-smoke-tied-time-low.aspx

Percentage of US Adults Who Smoke Cigarettes 1944-2012

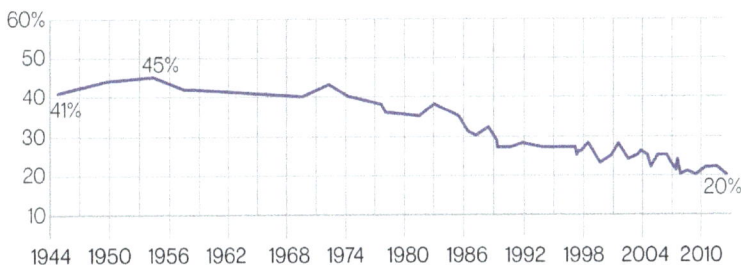

Americans seem to understand the risks of smoking better than citizens worldwide. The percentage of Americans who smoke is lower than most other nations, as seen in the image below.[5]

Annual Cigarettes Consumed per Capita Worldwide

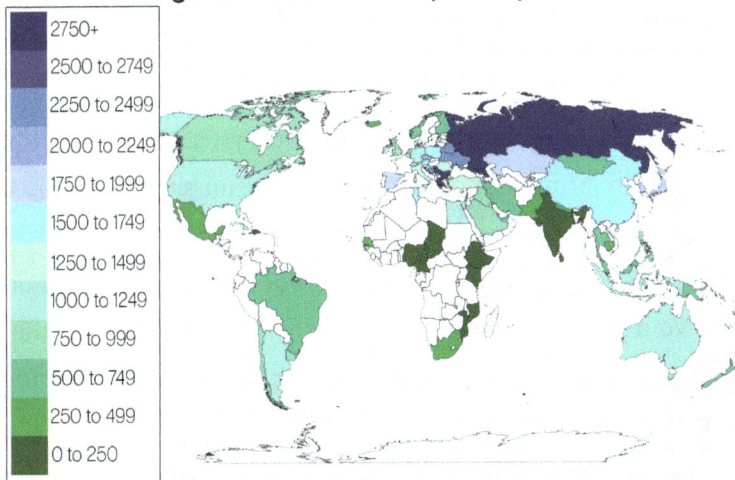

5 https://www.washingtonpost.com/news/worldviews/wp/2012/10/19/who-smokes-most-a-surprising-map-of-smoking-rates-by-country/?utm_term=.e5acba4ba153

would be to prevent people from smoking, drinking, becoming obese, and not exercising. While we're doing better in terms of smoking, obesity is on the rise. In fact, obesity hit a record high in 2015, as shown in the image below.[6] Preventative care is a pressing issue.

US Adult Obesity Rate, 2008-2015
Obesity Rate (BMI of 30+) among US adults, based on self-reported height and weight

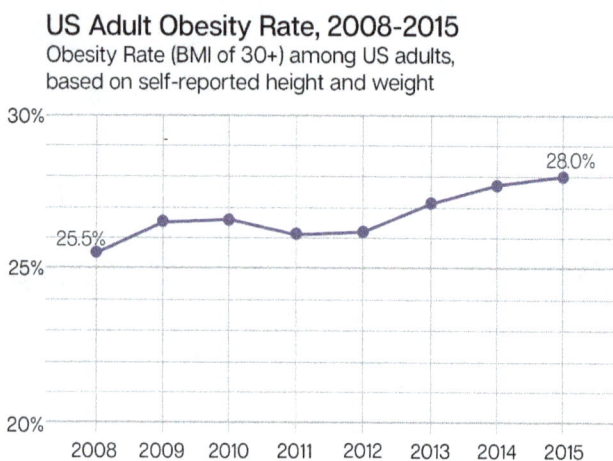

An increasing number of healthcare systems are currently investing in forms of preventative care. The missing puzzle piece here is how to engage physicians and give them an incentive to keep everyone healthy, since most of us are not paid to do so. We need to be innovative in the ways in which all stakeholders can share in the profits of health. This is the epitome of stakeholder alignment.

I am a lung cancer surgeon, which means that in the current healthcare system, I wouldn't make much if everyone had

---

6 http://www.gallup.com/poll/189182/obesity-rate-climbs-record-high-2015.aspx

stopped smoking thirty years ago. In that scenario, I'd have barely any patients to operate on. I'd still have a few, because patients develop lung cancer from exposure to asbestos and other environmental factors. An increasing number of patients get lung cancer, even though they've never smoked.

However, instead of hoping for people to need surgery, I could create a program to help every single person in New York City to stop smoking—and then get paid more each day for *not* performing surgery. We should incentivize the creation of programs that effectively reduce the incidence of lung cancer to such an extent that I would no longer need to perform as many operations. Many people reading this book are working on health-promoting programs like this.

These are the types of incentives we need to figure out. We need to develop a lucrative preventative care industry. Currently, the realistic approach to preventative care of chronic disease is to manage it before the patient develops the symptoms and complications that require hospital admission.

Yes, creating the ideal type of healthcare system that truly prevents the development of chronic disease would be very complicated—but that should be our ultimate goal.

In Conclusion

The goal is to provide every single American with health care while improving the quality of care and reducing costs. Improvements to the management of chronic disease will significantly advance the achievement of this goal.

Given the prevalence of chronic disease in the United States, it is imperative to the economic well-being of our healthcare system that we find more efficient ways to manage chronic conditions such as diabetes, heart disease, and obesity.

The lack of alignment among stakeholders within the healthcare industry clearly affects how well healthcare providers manage chronic disease. Our solutions must address alignment.

Regardless of what solutions we choose to implement, we'll need to take specific actions. The first action item is to accurately and fairly create a scoring system, devised and run by physicians, to assess the quality of care that patients with chronic disease are receiving. This will enable us to pinpoint areas that need improvement and single out programs that are working well. High-performing teams can be encouraged to share their protocols with low-performing teams.

Accurately measuring the quality of care and using appropriate metrics to measure treatment outcomes will enable us to move toward nationwide changes in the way we manage chronic disease. If we provide incentives for quality care and find ways to hold all stakeholders accountable for managing chronic disease, we will find ways to achieve more effective treatment plans and outcomes.

Patient engagement in their treatment must be established, and patients must be charged more for health care if they are not compliant with their diet, medicines, and exercise program.

Finally, as we further discuss in the next chapter, the fallacy of pre-existing conditions needs to be clearly identified. Liver failure from excessive drinking and emphysema from smoking a pack a day for forty years are not "pre-existing conditions" but rather "consequential conditions."

Chapter 8

PATIENTS MUST HAVE SKIN
IN THE GAME

A GREAT PORTION OF THIS BOOK HAS BEEN
dedicated to the exploration of the various ways in which we
can provide quality health care while lowering costs. Since
quality, cost, and value are closely related, it's essential that
all stakeholders agree upon a definition of healthcare value.
We need to measure the value of health care in ways that
actually improve quality and reduce costs. I have found that
few physicians and even hospital administrators understand
value—mainly because they are under so much pressure to
provide short-term results.

The average American patient does not question the value
of health care, but believes that he or she is entitled to the
best health care in the world, immediately, and without any

skin in the game—that is, without any financial obligation. Why should health care be different than any other high-end purchase we make every day? We don't all feel entitled to buy the most expensive car or house. We buy what we can afford, and we try to find the best value.

But health is different, isn't it? We all deserve high-quality health care, but we are not sure what defines value in health care or what the patient's responsibility for that care should be. Once the average patient has greater financial investment in the quality and cost of the care he or she is receiving, then the value of care will be better understood—including the value of the patient's own commitment to health.

In order to create a healthcare system that is invested in preventative care, provides quality care and treatment, is affordable for all stakeholders, and is accessible to everyone, we must measure value in terms of patient engagement. Patients should view health care as a right—and as I have repeatedly stated in this book, my viewpoint is that *every single American* should have access to high-quality care.

But patients should also realize that they have to take some ownership and responsibility for their own health. In fact, we can measure value by the level of responsibility patients take for their health. We can use metrics to measure patient engagement, including how regularly they make and keep doctor appointments, how well they comply with treatment recommendations, and whether they take their medications as prescribed—as well as their weight and exercise charts.

For our healthcare system to thrive, patients must be willing and active participants in their own treatment. We can promote this by creating a system in which patients are financially responsible for noncompliance and poor health choices. Essentially, what Americans pay for their healthcare needs to be based on the lifestyle choices they make.

An Unhealthy Understanding of Value

In the United States, there is an unhealthy perspective on value when it comes to health care. Patients believe that they should be able to receive what they want immediately, without any effort on their part. For example, many people say that they want to lose weight, but they can't—although they have not tried to change their diet or to exercise regularly. Instead, they ask their physicians for a pill or a gastric bypass operation.

To demonstrate the prevalence of this attitude, below are the estimated numbers of bariatric surgeries for the years indicated.[1] Bariatric surgery involves reducing the size of the stomach in order to achieve weight loss. It is true that most surgical programs also involve dietary and exercise elements, but they are usually feeble attempts.

Year	2011	2012	2013	2014	2015
Estimated number of surgeries	158,000	173,000	179,000	193,000	196,000

---

1 https://asmbs.org/resources/estimate-of-bariatric-surgery-numbers

People have developed a perception of the healthcare system as a resource that provides medication or procedures for instant gratification. This attitude does not allow for sustainable health, nor does it allow a productive healthcare system. A more holistic approach to health care and value would allow our system to invest in preventative care and engage all stakeholders, including patients. This shift in the understanding of value would significantly reduce healthcare costs.

National Fitness Tests

One method that can be used to determine appropriate healthcare premiums is to facilitate voluntary national fitness tests. Now, I know what that reader is thinking. I should disclose that I am a certified personal trainer and have my National Academy of Sports Medicine (NASM) certification. The culture in my home has always been to exercise daily, and all three of my boys work out. My wife died in 2013 from chemotherapy-induced leukemia from her breast cancer chemotherapy in 2010. While she was alive, we worked out as a family several times a week.

I am biased toward regular physical exercise. I know that, for most people, a voluntary system for exercise makes sense and will improve health.

In an ideal system, we would set up a standardized process for measuring health and lifestyle choices and then using this information to determine the amount of each patient's annual healthcare premium. When healthcare premiums are dependent upon patient behavior and on how well health and fitness are maintained, patients will be motivated to make better lifestyle choices. Preventative health care is based on such choices, and it is the key to improve our wellness and reduce healthcare costs.

Health insurance companies should be able to conduct fitness tests on the individuals covered by their healthcare plans. Every person would participate in a fitness test, and his or her doctor would use that information to set health goals. If the goals were met, premium costs would be reduced. These tests would be voluntary—people could choose to opt out—but we would need to set it up so that anyone who opts out of the fitness tests would automatically pay a higher premium. There would be various levels of the test based on age and other conditions such arthritis, knee pain, etc.

In this plan, a board of experts within the healthcare industry will create the metrics we use to measure a patient's health. Tests will then be administered each year during the designated testing period at national testing centers (school gymnasiums or the vast number of fitness centers could be put to this purpose), for which patients will pay a nominal fee. The majority of patients will participate, because participation will reduce their annual health insurance premiums.

If testing indicates improvement in the patient's overall health since the previous year, due to improved behavior (e.g., quitting drinking or smoking), or continued health as demonstrated by high scores, this will further lower their insurance premiums. The savings in the premiums would far exceed the patient's cost for opting into taking the test, and facilities will be aligned to offering the test, since they would collect a small fee as well.

As for gaming the system, cheap technology available today could be used to prevent this, such as: videotaping the test to ensure the instructor and patients were honest and requiring fingerprinting or others forms of identification, as we do at other standardized testing centers.

Overall health would be determined using a combination of metrics: heart rate, ability to exercise, body weight, body mass index, core strength, vision, and so forth. The standards would be easily adjusted as patients grow older. Various levels of fitness could be scored. These metrics, along with others, are strong indicators of a patient's current health and fitness level, which directly correlates with their future health.

One challenge in establishing this model is how it would deal with pre-existing conditions. This goes back to the significance of accurately collecting and analyzing data on disease, illness, health care, and treatment. We must be able to distinguish between conditions that directly relate to behavior and those that do not. We must also have accurate data on risk factors, red flags, and the costs of treatment.

If a patient can't complete the testing because of a pre-existing condition that is beyond their control, then they must not be charged a greater premium. The model proposed here is only to be applied to people who choose a lifestyle that is known to cause significant health problems. Those who are healthy will have the chance to reduce their health premiums by working hard to take of themselves.

Another challenge to implementing this model is the unfair advantage conferred by higher socioeconomic status in terms of maintaining health and fitness. For instance, many of my patients who were born into single-parent homes and lower economic backgrounds tend to get most of their nutrition from fast-food restaurants and are therefore predisposed to obesity. These patients have not been exposed to the culture my children have. They might not have the opportunity to join a gym and work out.

One solution to this problem would be for anyone under the age of eighteen who suffered from these socio-economic hardships to have the option to be exempt from the national fitness tests, or for every minor to be charged the same health-care premium. Those in great shape can opt into the fitness program so they can pay a lower premium. Those who were not afforded the opportunity to get in shape can fall into the national plan that provides them guaranteed health care.

However, once a patient reaches the age of eighteen or twenty-one or twenty-five, this might need to be adjusted. Should people in this age group be responsible for paying higher premiums if they choose to eat a poor diet, smoke, or not exercise? People turning eighteen who come from significantly poor economic backgrounds could be given a grace period for smoking, drinking, and obesity, or offered free participation in smoking cessation programs that exist in most every hospital in the USA.

Patients must take personal responsibility as adults so they have skin in the game. We can create accountability without creating a significant burden on patients. For example, we can also set limitations based on income, so that a patient earning minimum wage is not paying the same amount for a smoking-cessation program as a patient who earns a six-figure salary.

We must be a caring and understanding society that provides access to quality care for everyone—including access to preventative programs. We need to make sure those who did not have the same opportunity that my three boys have had can have an equal chance at a healthy life. But we must also hold people accountable for the choices they make, at some point in their life.

Cost of Complications

The proposed national fitness tests are necessary because the person who works out regularly, eats well, and maintains a low body- fat percentage should not be paying the same amount as the person who smokes, doesn't work out, and has a high body-fat percentage. Body mass index (BMI) is not an accurate reflection of fitness, since many body builders have high BMI but are in great cardio-vascular shape.

If we are to keep patients engaged in their health care, we need to accurately calculate the costs of treatment and care and give them an incentive to hit the gym daily or say no to that enticing piece of chocolate cake. For instance, what are the actual costs of smoking? Of obesity? The numbers are hard to calculate, but they are staggering.

For some people, the reality may be that they are obese but they still work every day, don't get sick, and don't need a heart bypass. If such a patient is obese without displaying symptoms or health concerns, he can argue that a higher healthcare premium is not fair or appropriate. The fact is, however, that obesity increases the patient's likelihood of developing specific health complications in the future and of having complications after surgery.

For example, one of the complications known to be associated with obesity is coronary artery disease. The direct medical costs of this condition put a heavy economic burden on our healthcare system.[2] About $26 billion is spent per year in the US on coronary artery bypass grafting, used to treat this disease.[3] Other lifestyle choices also can lead to predictable health problems—and predictable costs. If a patient develops fatty liver disease, often seen from alcohol abuse later in life, he might need a liver transplant, a procedure that costs nearly $600,000.[4]

These complications arise from the choices a patient makes over an extended period of time. If the patient chooses to run

2 https://www.ncbi.nlm.nih.gov/pubmed/9605051
3 http://www.medscape.com/viewarticle/434471_11
4 https://transplantliving.org/before-the-transplant/financing-a-transplant/the-costs/

these health risks, I believe he or she should also incur the financial risk associated with treatment.

The financial model proposed here is not new—in fact, it is similar to the models used for life and auto insurance. People who want life insurance can choose to smoke, but they are required to pay a higher premium for their life insurance. Similarly, people who have multiple speeding tickets or other moving violations can still obtain auto insurance—as long as they still have their driver's licenses—but they have to pay significantly more for coverage, because the insurance company knows that this kind of driver is likely to incur greater costs than one who has never been involved in an accident or received a ticket.

In other words, insurance companies calculate the costs of coverage based on risk factors, and they charge the insured accordingly. We can use the same model for health and wellness.

We know that, statistically, if an obese patient undergoes surgery, he or she is more likely to have a complication—a wound infection, a deep venous thrombosis, a blood clot, or pneumonia—not to mention that the operation is more difficult for the surgeon and anesthesiologists. The obesity means the patient is at greater risk of incurring higher medical costs. The premium paid should reflect that risk.

The conversation we need to have is about how to quantify these costs. We need to employ the models of insurance companies, which having been charging in this way for decades, but also find novel ways of applying those models to health care. We must find innovative ways to link national databases and insurance companies to create a healthcare model that promotes preventative care and reduces costs.

We also must take into account that, if we are to charge patients to have skin in the game, then we must provide them with more options and more easily obtained knowledge about their health care—especially patients who are underserved and underprivileged. Patients should be able to review healthcare providers the way we review insurance companies online. We can go to a website, put in our information, and then find the top five or ten companies that provide the insurance we're looking for. We can compare the price of each. Patients should be able to do this when they're looking for specialists, procedures, and other treatments. If we are asking patients to be financially accountable, then we must be accountable to them as well.

In Conclusion

In our current health insurance system, the healthy patient's premium often subsidizes the healthcare costs of a person who smokes or overeats. Insurance companies need the healthy person in the plan in order to help mitigate the risk. Our proposed solutions mandate the participation of the healthiest patients, but we believe they must be rewarded for their good choices by paying less. As a caring society, we want to give everyone equal access to health care—but not at the cost of patient accountability. As we have seen, patient accountability is one of the keys to solving our healthcare crisis.

This system of individualized premiums and fitness tests is similar to a taxation system, in that the people who use more of the resources need to pay more into it. We should set up the pay scale on a tiered system based on income, but it should also factor in lifestyle choices and overall fitness. We must be fair, but we must hold ourselves and one another accountable.

This may seem jarring to some people at first, but analyzing financial risk and charging accordingly is not new. Drivers are charged varying premium rates based on their age, zip code, prior accidents, and how many tickets they've received. Our healthcare system can provide better quality care at lower costs if we employ a similar insurance system.

Many details of this system will need to be worked out, but the important first step is to get these ideas to the table so that stakeholders and leaders in the medical community can collaborate. In my experience, money motivates people in a way that other things don't. Although most of us also are motivated by concepts much greater than money, money helps create alignment.

Unfortunately, more people are motivated by money than by the idea of robust health. Because of this, the changes proposed in this chapter may result in a much healthier America.

The important thing is that we acknowledge the need to engage patients and ensure that all stakeholders have skin in the game. We will see great improvements to our healthcare system once patients feel a sense of ownership of their own health.

Chapter 9

BENEFITING FROM INNOVATION

ONE OF THE MAIN COMPONENTS TO SOLVING our healthcare crisis is the call for innovative ideas and methods. In Chapter 1, we saw that the current state of our healthcare system has been in the making for decades. The challenges we are experiencing are not new, which means that we can only find solutions by thinking of and trying new approaches.

One way to find solutions that increase quality and reduce costs is by connecting big data with entrepreneurs. New businesses are attracted by the potential income in health care and the relatively high profit margins. There are many ways we can help health care benefit from innovation, if we continue evolving our approach. New ways of thinking can create positive change. This chapter covers some innovative approaches and new ideas that will serve as examples.

Twisting

The examples in this section demonstrate *twisting*, the relatively new notion of taking an idea from one industry and applying it to another. Many of us have been inspired to apply a concept used in one sector to a problem in a completely different sector.

When I first started working at the University of Alabama, Birmingham, no one was distributing or collecting patient surveys. I initiated a survey program at UAB and—in line with what I previously detailed—I found that the biggest complaints my patients and their family members had was the hospital food. I went to a couple of nearby restaurants and contracted with the owners to deliver special meals to hospital patients at a reduced price. The hospital didn't profit from this at all, but it had a remarkable effect on patients. They acted as if I had brought in private chefs just to serve them!

About six months after implementing this, a nurse supervisor admonished me for bringing in outside food. Hospital administration began to fear legal issues, and I was asked to terminate the deal I had set up with these local eateries.

I had tried to solve a problem by moving forward with an innovative approach—but the hospital (understandably) recognized a potential risk I hadn't seen, and shut this innovation down very quickly. This is why we must be willing to keep evolving our approach. The old way of thinking was not solving these problems, but we were learning a great deal through trying new ideas.

Now, fifteen years later, UAB has magnets they place outside each patient's room that indicate whether they are participating in a special meal program or the basic one, and if the family members visiting also have opted for special food. While it took more than a decade for hospital leadership to realize that providing patients with poor quality food and no options was a problem, they eventually came up with a solution very similar to the one that I had implemented.

My idea had been by no means brilliant, but it was innovative and had quickly solved a problem. We must be flexible and open to new ways of thinking about a problem. The hospital could have been providing this service to patients for years, but it took them more than a decade to circle back to the starting point.

Another example is one I have faced during my time at New York University, and it concerns a problem we have examined before: patient discharge times. But this time, we're trying to resolve a discharge problem from the patient's point of view.

Patients might have written orders to be discharged by eight a.m., but they don't actually leave the hospital until four p.m. One reason is that it's hard for family members to get into the congested city to pick up their loves ones. City traffic delays lead to a bottleneck in the hospital, which means patients in the recovery room cannot get out to the floor, and then patients cannot go into the operating room to have surgery because there are no recovery room beds.

We are trying to partner with industry and ride-share services like Uber or Lyft—or other "non-siren" ambulance services—to help get patients home. In this scenario, the hospital will pay for the car ride, which averages around $15.00.[1] In exchange for picking up this fare, the hospital can admit a new patient, whose medical treatments generate an average of $2,000 for the hospital each day.[2] It's good for the hospital's bottom line, but more importantly, it provides a valuable service to the patient and family members. Everyone benefits from improved hospital throughput.

Customer service is a problem that health care has ignored for too long. Yes, we have to be good, caring doctors first. If we are surgeons, we have to be able to cut and sew and dissect. But in general, patients are our customers—and most hospitals do not provide good customer service.

For those who read this and disagree, please tell me: Where else do you pay money so that your hosts can give you an ugly, ill-fitting uniform, assign you a number, put you in an uncomfortable bed, and cause you pain? It sounds more like a prison than a hospital!

These examples demonstrate how we can reduce costs and provide a higher quality of care, by being flexible and welcoming innovation. Offering the option of special food—and using

1 https://www.nerdwallet.com/blog/insurance/number-rides-pay-insurance-lyft-uber/
2 http://www.beckershospitalreview.com/finance/average-cost-per-inpatient-day-across-50-states.html

ride-share services to get patients home—are examples of ways we can apply technological advancements to meet our healthcare needs. This is *twisting* at its best.

The Future with Apps

Online and mobile applications are going to be a big part of the innovations that shape the future of health care. Apps on the market today can actually enable you to do your own EKG with your phone and send it to your doctor. We now have the capability to add some plug-ins to our phones, download an app, and hook ourselves up to a device with which we can interrogate a pacemaker. Soon, you might be able to take an ultrasound of your abdomen—all from the comfort of your home.

The scan or exam you take can be transmitted instantly to your doctor—who *also* is at home—so it can be reviewed. Then your doctor can use Face Time or Skype with you to explain the diagnosis and come up with a treatment plan.

It's becoming increasingly clear that apps will be the key to innovation in the healthcare industry, improving quality and lowering costs. These solutions might prevent people from needing to be readmitted to the hospital and will help enable preventative care by providing immediate intervention. Apps will become an increasingly large part of medicine.

One of the projects I'm involved with in New York City is a telemedicine clinic. Telemedicine enables us to evaluate and diagnose patients without them coming into the office, because we do it over the phone. Of course, we're not able to deliver a lung resection to your house—at least not yet—but we are certainly able to facilitate more outpatient care, which reduces costs by cutting down hospital visits. The future of telemedicine is phone, Skype, FaceTime, and similar services and apps. Technology will allow us to look at wounds and surgical incisions, as well as to conduct check-ins and follow-up appointments remotely.

We are already able to insert a chip into someone's arm or calf that collects all the medical information a physician or hospital would need. These chips contain information on blood type, allergies, recent surgeries, and so on. Our future is not electronic health care records (EHR) software, but rather digital chips in every patient.

Upon entry into an emergency room or a hospital for any procedure, a patient will be scanned with a hand-held wand. No matter where their previous operations or care may have been, the information will be included on the chip. Physicians will no longer have to wait for files to be faxed over from another office or other hospitals. All of the pertinent information will be in the patient's chip—including x-rays and scan results.

We already use microchips on pets—now it's time to take advantage of this technology for patients. Microchips would revolution medical records and eliminate some of the time doctors and nurses spend charting. Having this information readily available could be extremely helpful in emergency situations, when a patient is unable to tell doctors their medical history.

One possible drawback to microchips is that they might make it harder to keep sensitive medical information private.

It's possible that someone might develop the capability to scan your information or monitor you as you walk down the street. Concern of possible HIPPA (federal patient privacy) regulations has slowed down the progress needed to make microchipping patients a reality.

Technological advances will soon make it possible for doctors to monitor a patient's post-op heart rate, temperature, and blood pressure wirelessly from the doctor's phone. This will cut down on the time physicians have to spend making rounds to follow up on patients, freeing them to spend more time seeing patients who still need care.

This technology is already prevalent in our society: smart watches and Fitbit can transmit the patient's heart rate, blood pressure, and temperature wirelessly. If we could transmit data from these devices to our physicians before we called them, remote check-ins would be easy. Then the physician could decide whether we needed to come into the office for further testing. This is quality care at significantly reduced cost.

Post-op Changes

Surgeons must follow strict guidelines and protocols when a patient has an operation. Most of my surgical colleagues see all of their patients again two to three weeks after surgery; about 99 percent of patients at these visits have no real problems.

I have argued for years that the routine post-op checkup visit provides little value to anyone. The patient has to travel to the office, park the car, and then wait to tell the doctor they are feeling well and that the incisions look great—exactly as we would have expected. I have essentially eliminated post-operative visits in my practice. When the patient is home, they can show me the incision over the phone. We call them a week after surgery to give them the final pathology results and ask for digital photos of the incisions.

It is important to note that technology will not change the protocols for treating any patients who *do* have problems after surgery, but eliminating unnecessary outpatient visits for the patients recovering nicely will enable doctors to provide faster and more efficient care for patients who really need them. The patient who can access us immediately via Face Time—rather than waiting for a clinic visit the next morning—gives us a better chance to troubleshoot potential problems immediately. Technology and innovation will improve post-op recovery and reduce complications.

Incentives for Innovation

To increase the amount of innovation we are currently experiencing in the healthcare industry, we should find ways to reward companies that introduce new methods, processes, and tools. Because we know the greatest motivator is a financial reward, we can begin by enticing companies with less regulatory red tape. We can consider providing tax incentives, like those that have prompted innovation in solar and wind energy sources over the past several years as well as other incentives. Recognition can also be used as incentive—for example, through industry-wide competitions and awards.

It is likely that, in the future, all of the companies that are innovating in the healthcare industry are going to be purchased by large hospital networks and healthcare systems. With access to greater funds and mass production, we will then witness how their technology and other innovations affect patients and healthcare providers on the ground level.

This will give patients more skin in the game, because they are going to be engaged in their own health care and their own data collection in an entirely new way. They will feel more empowered to carefully evaluate the physicians and surgeons they turn to for care. Patients, hospitals, insurance companies, and doctors alike will all be able to measure one another, which will help improve quality.

One question concerning these apps and devices is whether everyone will have access to them and will be able to utilize them to their full potential. Realistically, we know that we are not going to be able to provide equal access for everyone, since access depends so much on location, economic background, and other factors.

We will not be able to eliminate this country's tiered healthcare system in the next ten years, but we can strive to make health care more like a commercial airline flight—although those in the first class section might have a more enjoyable overall experience, all patients will get the same pilots, all will leave and land at the same time, and all will arrive safely at the destination.

If devices such as smart phones are to become part of the healthcare system, protocols must be established to provide some level of equal access to basic devices. For instance, patients could be given the devices they need and then asked to return them when their treatment is complete. Of course, this runs this risk of loss, theft, or damage to expensive equipment, but we can explore ways to hold patients accountable and insure devices to avoid financial loss.

It may be possible for devices to be available by prescription, in which case insurance companies would cover the majority of the cost. Insurance companies might approve this process once we collect data showing the cost benefits of patient access to such devices.

Will devices compromise patient privacy? We must find a way to allow patients to see when their information is being viewed and by whom. It is important to recognize that, any time we are collecting data, protecting privacy is a top priority. In this case, it may be a priority that companies will invest in; the same companies creating innovative technology and techniques can and will devise protective measures to keep that technology safe.

Can data from devices be trusted for accuracy? If patients are paying for their health care based on their behavior, we can assume that some people will try to cheat by falsifying the information transmitted from such devices. For example, some people may take the watch off their arm and strap it on a friend who is in better shape and doesn't drink.

We will need to find ways to prevent people from cheating. Because a device like the Fitbit allows us to measure someone's heart rate and blood pressure, it would likely be obvious if the device was on someone else's wrist. We could even implement ways to make sure the data we collect is specific to the individual we're measuring, such as requiring fingerprint or other types of scanning. The most important thing to focus on first is creating these innovations and putting them to use.

In Conclusion

Many new apps and technologies represent breakthrough innovations, and some are already in use that will be useful in health care. Making these devices available to the public for medical purposes will lower costs and improve the quality of health care we deliver. We want to start this process by ensuring that companies that come up with innovations like these (or make them more accessible or more cost-efficient) are rewarded.

It is also important that we document the innovations that are working and share them with others in the industry, so that we can all benefit. When we create best practices, update protocols, or create innovative processes, we need to share this information in industry-specific forums, just as we do currently do in scientific meetings.

The tech industry, for example, has several competitions every year in which individuals and small companies compete to win money and recognition for their innovative methods, processes, or devices. We can introduce more programs that spark innovation and promote sharing within the medical industry. What we need now is a call for innovative ideas, techniques, and methods.

Chapter 10

HEALTH SAVINGS ACCOUNTS

THE IMPLEMENTATION OF NOVEL IDEAS WILL enable us to achieve the stakeholder alignment necessary to solve our healthcare crisis. Previous chapters explored current resources, such as big data and metrics, that we are not yet utilized to their full potential. The potential of health savings accounts (HSAs) is often overlooked. HSAs or similar plans will play a major role in the solution to our healthcare situation.

HSAs are not a new idea, but they're an underutilized resource. Many people don't enroll in these plans because of the limitations and stipulations they carry. For example, HSAs are currently only available to people who have high-deductible health plans. Why? As I have suggested earlier in this book, this regulatory rule need to be changed. Health Savings Accounts should be available to all Americans who work—just like an IRA or a 457 plan.

HSAs were established in 2003 by the federal government as part of the Medicare Prescription Drug Improvement and Modernization Act, to allow individuals enrolled in high-deductible health plans to receive tax-preferred treatment of funds designated for medical expenses.[1] Don't let this governmental mumbo jumbo confuse you! Just stick with the upcoming definitions to fully understand how HSAs work, because their role in solving our national healthcare problem will be important.

I find the easiest way to understand HSAs is to compare them to other savings accounts, such as IRAs and 529 plans. People can use special savings accounts to put money away for retirement (IRS) or a kid's college tuition (529 plan). While those accounts provide tax benefits for specific types of costs, an HSA does the same thing for medical costs.

Those who qualify can open an HSA through their employer or on their own. They can set up the account with one sole beneficiary or include spouses and dependents up to the age of twenty-six. HSAs offer many benefits—the contributions to this savings account are not taxed, or are tax deductible, and funds in an HSA account can accumulate interest without tax. It sounds like an IRA, doesn't it?

This chapter includes information on high-deductible health insurance plans and an assessment of the pros and cons of HSAs today. Understanding the strengths and weaknesses

---

1 https://www.treasury.gov/resource-center/faqs/Taxes/Pages/Health-Savings-Accounts.aspx

of these plans enables us to identify areas for improvement and more fully utilize their benefits.

High-deductible Health Insurance Plans

High-deductible health insurance plans allow people access to healthcare insurance with lower monthly premium payments.[2] Remember, the deductible is the amount you have to pay out of your pocket when you get a bill. The insurance only kicks in when your medical bills exceed the amount of your deductible.

In essence, you gamble a bit when you have a high-deductible policy. You can say, I don't think I'll get sick this year, so I want to pay as little per month as I can. That will reduce my monthly fee—but if I *do* get sick, I'll have to pay much more before my insurance kicks in.

Car insurance offers plans with high deductibles. Many car insurance plans that charge a low annual cost have a $1,000 deductible—that's the amount you must pay in full toward having a broken windshield repaired before the insurance company covers the remainder of the related costs. You can choose to enroll in a plan that does not have a deductible, so that the insurance company will cover the entire cost, but you will pay a higher monthly fee for this coverage.

As HSAs were created to offer tax benefits to individuals with high-deductible plans, you can only qualify for an HSA

2 A deductible is the amount paid for healthcare costs out of pocket prior to the insurance company assuming financial responsibility

if you are enrolled in a high-deductible healthcare plan. This is an important point and one that I hope we can alter in the future, but for now, you have to have a high deductible plan in order to apply.

The definition of a "high-deductible healthcare plan" is determined each year, and may change from one year to the next. In both 2016 and 2017, the minimum annual deductible for individuals in high-deductible plans was $1,300, or $2,600 for families. The out-of-pocket[3] maximum was $6,550 for individuals and $13,100 for families.[4]

These numbers are interesting because they reveal the reality of enrolling in high-deductible health insurance plans. They are a way of gambling that you won't experience any catastrophic health issues and actually need to use your health insurance. This may be a lucrative gamble for healthy individuals between the ages of twenty-one and sixty-five, but the risk increases with age—and people of all ages are subject to unexpected illnesses and accidents.

The Potential Strengths of HSAs

Preferential Tax Treatment of Funds

HSAs enable pre-tax contributions for healthcare costs, which can be automatically deducted through employer payroll

---

3 Out-of-pocket maximum is the greatest amount a patient can be required to spend on healthcare costs, including copayments, deductibles, co-insurance, etc. before the insurance company covers all costs.

4 https://www.optumbank.com/individuals-families/hsa-eligibility.html

or paid directly to the company by the individual, similar to a private healthcare insurance plan. Contributions to HSAs avoid federal income tax and are not taxed by most states, either. Funds that are used directly from the HSA to cover the costs of healthcare expenses remain tax-free.

If you make $5,000 a month, your tax rate is applied to those earnings. But if you pay $1,000 monthly into an HSA, your tax rate will be applied only to the $4,000 that is left. In essence, the HSA lets you pay for medical expenses with pre-tax or tax-free dollars.

It is important to note that, when you use an HSA, you need to keep track of all of your expenditures, contributions, and receipts to prove these were real medical expenses. You might have to pay for medical expenses out of pocket and be reimbursed, once per month, based on the receipts you submit. Because keeping track can be a challenge, some companies have simplified this process and now offer HSA debit cards

Some employers offering HSAs as part of their benefits package also match employee contributions—similar to employers matching via 401(k) retirement plans—and this money is again untaxed for the individual. Contributions to HSAs can also be made with after-tax dollars. The advantage here is that the amount that is contributed is then tax deductible.

HSA funds also grow tax-free. The funds in an HSA can accumulate interest and continue to grow, untaxed. That's why it might be helpful to think of a healthcare savings account as an IRA for healthcare spending instead of for spending in your retirement.

Annual Rollover

Funds in HSAs also continue to grow from one year to the next. In individual healthcare savings plans, there is no stipulation that the funds must be used within the same fiscal year in which they have been deposited. Funds accrue interest and remain tax free from one year to the next, and account funds can build on themselves throughout the year. Some employers or companies will only offer HSA plans that must be used within the year—but if you have an HSA in your own name, the funds can roll over. This is an important point and one that I suggest that we make available to all US citizens via their employer.

Coverage Variety

HSAs not only cover the obvious costs one thinks of as health care—like emergency room visits, operations, etc.—may also cover the costs of a multitude of different healthcare needs. For instance, chiropractic care, acupuncture, substance abuse treatment, service animals, wheelchairs, hearing aids, prescription drugs, and psychiatric care are all covered by HSA funds—and so are home healthcare items such as bandages and aspirin.

The Potential Weaknesses of HSAs

Neglecting Preventative Care

As we've established that the best way to save money in health care is to provide preventative care, it is a potential weakness that HSAs are only offered to individuals with high-deductible plans. High-deductible plans do not incentivize preventative care, since many people do not want to pay out of pocket for annual check-ups and regular visits. Instead, many individuals with high-deductible plans only use their healthcare insurance for catastrophic issues. Removing the requirement to be enrolled in a high-deductible plan will resolve this issue.

We also suggest that HSAs could be used for preventative care programs. Think of how powerful it would be for patients to pay, with pre-tax dollars, to enroll in smoking cessation plans—especially if the only way they can get that money pre-tax is to spend it on such programs.

Forced to Save

Americans generally are not good savers, and this can be an obstacle to utilizing the potential of HSAs. In fact, Medicare was set up because Americans are bad at saving. Medicare was established to ensure that people have health coverage in retirement by pulling funds directly from their earnings, long before retirement, because Americans were not setting aside funds for themselves. HSAs essentially force you to save your money and give you pre-taxed dollars to do it. **And best of all, you—not the government—get to decide how and where to spend it.** People with high-deductible healthcare plans need to have savings to cover that deductible, and HSAs simplify that process.

Medicare Disqualification

Individuals on Medicare cannot be enrolled in an HSA. I suggest we amend this rule and make Medicare an option, and then make HSAs another option. Unfortunately, it is currently not possible to opt out of Medicare—and this is one reason I proposed earlier in this book that opting out should be possible.

If it were possible for individuals to opt out of Medicare, individuals sixty-five and older would be able to enroll in an HSA if they chose to do so. They could manage the money themselves. Who cares about your money more—you, or the government?

Contribution Limit

Individuals can make contributions to their HSAs for the previous year up to April 15 of each year. Still, regulations limit the amount that can be contributed to an HSA. As of 2017, the maximum amount is $3,400 for individuals and $6,750 per family.[5] For individuals who are fifty-five and older, the contribution limit is increased by $1,000 each year. I suggest these limits be at least doubled if not tripled.

Financial Risk

The major disadvantage to enrolling in a high-deductible healthcare plan is that you will pay much more out of pocket if you have an unexpected illness or injury that requires medical

---

5 https://www.shrm.org/resourcesandtools/hr-topics/benefits/pages/irs-sets-2017-hsa-contribution-limits.aspx

attention, lab tests, hospital admission, or specialists. If you are not able to cover the difference between what you have in your HSA and your maximum deductible, it will be a financial burden. You can, of course, add more funds to your HSA and then deduct those contributions from your taxes—but if you don't have the funds to add, these plans may not be the option for you at this time.

Innovation

HSAs have the potential to provide more people with quality care at lower costs, though there are currently some obstacles to fully taking advantage of an HSA. We need to collaborate and implement innovative changes that help individuals realize the full potential of HSAs. For example, we can find a solution to offset the financial risk associated with enrolling in a high-deductible health insurance plan.

Insurance companies can offer small, low-interest loans to offset the cost of unexpected injury or illness. I refer to these loans as *catastrophic health insurance plans that supplement the HSAs.* For instance, if an individual spent more than $3,000 in a year and used funds from the HSA, the *catastrophic health insurance* could provide an additional $3,550 to cover the difference between the HSA funds and the annual out-of-pocket maximum.

These plans could be set up so that individuals pay a small amount into it regularly and can use it in the case of a catastrophic health issue. Even better, insurance companies via a free market are the ones best able to assess the cost of these plans. The free market would create competition to these supplemental plans and the lower costs would win.

Essentially, these plans would supplement HSAs and minimize the risk of enrolling in such a plan. Generally, individuals who enroll in HSAs are healthy, which is why they risk the high-deductible plan. Insurance companies want healthy people enrolled in their plans because this population is more profitable to them and helps mitigate the risk of older patients—and, as described at length in this book, this helps to spread risk amongst a heterogeneous population and keep prices down. This is an example of a novel idea that will benefit individuals and align stakeholders.

In Conclusion

As leaders in the healthcare industry, it is our responsibility to have conversations about the strengths and weaknesses of our healthcare system, so that we can implement solutions that truly align stakeholders and provide quality care and low cost. Some solutions will need to be novel.

It is often the implementation of novel ideas or disruptive technology that creates sustainable change. The HSA is not necessarily a novel idea at this point, but it hasn't been used enough or in the optimal manner. We can all benefit from some creative adjustments. The end result will be increased patient engagement, which will lead to better treatment outcomes at lower cost.

Getting patients to decide where and how they spend their own money on their health is one great way to increase engagement, especially if they're given the option to spend pre-tax money. When patients are saving their money with tax benefits, and choosing when and how to spend these funds, they are going to approach their health care with a higher level of engagement and be much more involved in decision-making.

Fully engaged patients will finally be asking, "What does that cost, do I really need it, and are you the right doctor to give it to me?" Remember, as described in Chapter 3, when patients ask this question every day, we are on our way to solving our healthcare problem. Making HSAs available to a greater portion of the population might produce extraordinary results.

Chapter 11

FINAL THOUGHTS

THE UNITED STATES HAS THE HIGHEST QUALITY healthcare system in the world, for those who can afford it. Does it offer the best value—that is, the best quality for the least cost? Probably not. But the quality element is there, and it keeps getting better. We do not need a complete overhaul of the American healthcare system—nor can we afford one.

While this book did not address different educational systems across the world, I believe we in the USA are by far the best at teaching the art and science of medicine and surgery. This does not mean that our system is perfect, or even the best in all aspects of education. There is room for improvement in many areas, and we can learn from other countries' systems that are superior to ours in many ways. Some of these areas have been identified in this book, along with possible solutions that, if implemented, would create sustainable solutions to our healthcare crisis.

Our overall goal must be to establish stakeholder alignment in order to provide every American with access to quality health care at affordable costs.

The main obstacles to achieving this goal stem from the highly politicized nature of our healthcare system. Multiple players have billions of dollars at risk, and if the rules of the game are changed even a little, many will suffer immensely. But change is the nature of all sectors, including health care. Those who do not change and evolve will perish.

Our political culture today is non-productive. The mutual distrust between Democrats and Republicans and the current narrative creates an atmosphere that is not conducive to collaboration. This situation is an embarrassment to me, personally, as I travel the world and operate and/or lecture on the worlds stage and hear the comments about our current leadership.

We need collaboration between the two major parties, and we need leadership that takes on challenges with a solutions-oriented approach—not sophomoric name-calling. We need to stop the silly politics that delay change and endanger those who need health care.

The solutions to our healthcare problem include policy change, stakeholder alignment, database communication, patient engagement, accurate metrics, and implementing new health insurance and savings plans.

Final Thoughts

Until our leadership can take ownership of these problems and check politics at the door, we will never be able to delve into possible new solutions. But I believe we can and will eventually overcome the challenges we face, if we can rise above politics concerning our healthcare system and pass effective legislation.

We cannot eliminate the differences in the quality of care available at different prices, because health care is a commodity, just like airfare, clothing, cars, and nearly every other purchase. A two-tiered system exists in the US for most everything, and this is likely to include health care for a long-time—no matter what we do.

But healthcare can be like air travel. The main metrics or the endpoints—such as the time you take off, the time you land, the skill of your pilot, and the safety of the trip—are the same for all passengers, although we all know that the experience is quite different for those in the first class seats, compared to those sitting in coach.

The treatment of illness and disease should be the same. The medicines—their safety, efficacy, and availability—as well as the five-year survival rates for the disease should be the same for all patients, irrespective of their socio-economic status. However, their experience may be a bit different.

We can use big data to create metrics that drive the type of behavior that guarantees a basic quality of care for every patient. It is our responsibility to ensure that the basic level of care is competent, patient-centric, and available to everyone—because that is what the United States represents. If we are a loving and caring society, we must take care of *everyone*—not just those who can afford help.

One necessity, if we are to improve our healthcare system, is to reduce government involvement in health care. An example is the veterans' healthcare system, as discussed in Chapter 2. We need to allow individual states and other geographic sectors to problem-solve and implement novel ways that will work for them and their culture. We need government to help subsidize those patients who cannot get other forms of health care. Free markets will force innovation and lower costs, and it will help us advance on the road to solutions in health care.

We also need to ensure that patients have more skin in the game by changing the way we engage patients and requiring some level of patient financial investment. Along the same lines, we should ensure that patients have access to more information on procedures, treatments, hospitals, physicians, surgeons, and best practices in general.

Patients should also have more options when it comes to their health care. This will force us, as providers, to improve our game at lower costs. Patients with more financial investment will expect more choices, and once they exercise their right to choose, they'll be more engaged in their own health care. This means the patient, as well as we the doctors, will ask about the cost and necessity of treatment, surgery, tests, and other procedures. Patient engagement will undoubtedly lower costs while improving outcomes, because it will force us, as healthcare providers, to improve our quality while simultaneously reducing our costs.

Improving health care will require the necessity of innovation—this cannot be stressed enough. The force to innovate is lessened when current ways of doing things are federally subsidized. People must come up with new ways to deliver care—and people will, if they're properly incentivized. We can use technological advancements, social networking, telecommunications, and the internet—along with other tools—to improve the quality of care that we provide while increasing the level of patient engagement and reducing costs.

Innovation and cooperation are the keys to achieving these goals.

* 9 7 8 1 9 4 7 3 6 8 3 8 5 *